GOD'S
TROUBLEMAKERS

GOD'S TROUBLEMAKERS

HOW WOMEN OF FAITH
ARE CHANGING THE WORLD

Katharine Rhodes Henderson

continuum

NEW YORK • LONDON

2006

The Continuum International Publishing Group Inc
80 Maiden Lane, New York, NY 10038

The Continuum International Publishing Group Ltd
The Tower Building, 11 York Road, London SE1 7NX

Printed in the United States of America

Library of Congress Cataloging-in-Publication Data

Henderson, Katharine Rhodes.
    God's troublemakers : how women of faith are changing the world / Katharine Rhodes.
      p.   cm.
    Includes bibliographical references and index.
    ISBN-13: 978-0-8264-1867-8 (hardcover : alk. paper)
    ISBN-10: 0-8264-1867-8 (hardcover : alk. paper)
    1. Women and religion. 2. Women – Religious life. I. Title. II. Title: God's trouble makers.
    BL458.H46 2006
    200.82 – dc22

                                         2006016049

CONTENTS

PREFACE

"Wade in the water. Wade in the water, children. Wade in the water, God's gonna trouble the waters." The familiar words and tune of this spiritual came to me as I was working on a cover concept and title for this book. Counterintuitive though it may seem initially, "troubling the waters" has a positive connotation, suggesting that no matter how mired in the status quo the world may seem or "stuck" we may be in our personal lives, God is at work doing a new thing if we but perceive it. But God is not the only one doing the "troubling." As we become God's hands and feet we too are troublemakers, making changes that may start small but can emanate in ever widening circles.

For some people writing a book is a solitary pursuit; for others of us it is a product of "the village," the community of family, friends, and colleagues who help midwife it to birth. First, I thank the women whose lives inspired me to write this book and who entrusted me with their words and stories. Dr. Sharon McDade, my dissertation advisor, kept pressing me forward in the initial stages. Karen Thorkilsen brought her extraordinary expertise to the project as a professional editor, and she became a provocative conversation partner and friend. She kept the faith about the importance of this book when I could not keep it for myself. At a strategic juncture Barbara Dobkin urged me to take myself — both more and less seriously — with support that allowed me writing time and editorial help. For her vision of what women can do to change the world and for her friendship over the years, I am deeply grateful. Linda Gottlieb is the best wordsmith I know, brilliant and irreverent. When I shared my musings and concepts about the book title with her at a cocktail party, Linda was able to whip up the edgy term "God's Troublemakers" that seemed just right. Bob Hartman did equal justice to the book cover. Frank Oveis, the Senior Editor at Continuum International Publishing Group, personifies wisdom and wit. I cannot imagine having a more wonderful companion in the publishing process. Barbara Wheeler, Lee Hancock, Daniel Brenner, Macky Alston, Eileen Macholl, Patricia Washington, Lisa Anderson, Sharon Miller, Robert Reber, and other colleagues at Auburn are a community of support and rich conversation rarely experienced in a work environment.

During the process of researching this book, I was profoundly changed. With their lives and stories the women leaders urged me to find my "public" work. Face to Face / Faith to Faith was born through partnership with Melodye Feldman, who has become a trusted colleague and friend and whose willingness to engage "the other" deeply, including me, has made me a more authentic person. Face to Face/Faith to Faith would not have been possible without the support of Mark Hostetter and Alix Habib, who shared the vision from the beginning and were willing to launch it. We are grateful for the many others who have joined them since. I want to thank the students of Face to Face / Faith to Faith, who courageously move forward in the face of violence, tragedy, and loss to practice understanding, forgiveness, and peace.

Friends are an antidote to despair and burnout — that is one of the learnings from the women in this book. The deft coaching and friendship of Barbara Moss and Ellen McGrath have prompted me to see more clearly and to make connections that are the sustaining lifelines. Taya Thurman, Betsy Kovacs, Holley Bishop, Paula Hawkins, and many others continued to love me despite my unavailability while writing this book.

And finally, there is family. I dedicate this book to my parents, Lela Nelson and Arnold Black Rhodes, whose knowledge of God's love and commitment to justice, have shaped me inescapably, and to Chuck, my heart's delight, and our children, Julia, Andrew, and Kirsten.

Chapter 1

SILENCE IS AN ACT

If Eve, the first woman God ever made, was strong enough to turn the world upside down alone, the women of today ought to be able to get it right side up again! — Sojourner Truth, 1851

How do you create a life of meaning? What motivates people to try to change the world? When faced with injustice, why do some people walk away, while others stop, respond, and act? Does one individual's life matter? How can one person be a force for good? What, if anything, does God have to do with it?

These questions have been the driving force for my own life since my earliest years, and the source of many sleepless nights. I am not alone. As a minister and educator, I have been listening for over two decades to countless individuals who are haunted and challenged by these questions too. We live in an era when they press at us with particular urgency. Yet even as our response seems to matter more, we may harbor deep doubts about whether it will be "enough." Now that the stage is so obviously global and numbingly complex, it is all the more difficult to imagine how a sole actor can make a difference.

Historically, faith traditions have been a source of inspiration for courageous social action. But lately we have been seeing a great deal of the dark side of religion. Fundamentalists turned terrorists. Clergy as sexual abusers. We have been seeing the dark side of secularism too, itself a form of faith. Capitalism without a conscience. Accountants and CEOs as con men. Stock price as God.

1

What's missing are compelling stories of ethical leadership in the public realm. These we have not heard widely since the 1960s, when the Civil Rights movement demonstrated how religious conviction and public commitment can work together on behalf of the public good. Earlier, figures like Martin Luther King Jr., Gandhi, Dorothy Day, and Sojourner Truth developed this tradition. More recently, the fusion of these forces has been seen in public figures like Jimmy Carter, Bishop Desmond Tutu, and Nelson Mandela.

For the most part, however, contemporary religion in America has been preoccupied internally with institutional survival and relevance. While the Religious Right has become more vocal and strident, the progressive middle and left have grown silent, and for many, faith has become privatized, something best kept to oneself and on the periphery of public life. Religious moderates and liberals have appropriated this code of silence in order to operate more fully in a secular context, and to avoid being dismissed as religious fanatics.

Flying toward Full Disclosure

Let me give you a personal example. Parallel rifts on the theme could be reported by any religious professional. When a stranger next to me on an airplane or at a cocktail party asks what I do, I must decide how much of my religious self to reveal. The safest answer I can give is "an educator and administrator." If I add that this occurs in a seminary, it may set off an internal discourse: "Did she say seminary (what exactly is that?) or cemetery?" If I am going for full disclosure, I say "Presbyterian minister whose primary ministry happens in a seminary."

Divulging to someone that you are an ordained minister is a Rorschach test of sorts that can elicit a wide range of responses. Some people, I sense, are launched into an immediate scan of our previous conversation to see if they have said anything that might offend me, or worse, cause their eternal damnation. For them, "minister" means "moral authority who stands in judgment" — the behavior police. Usually a conversation stopper. But for others, "minister" is a conversation opener. "Minister" is someone comfortable with subjects not usually discussed but often begging to be aired — fear of death, the wonder of birth, personal secrets, ethical dilemmas, the mystery of why we are here. If I do not use the word "minister," I have not signaled my conviction that we all can — and should — talk about such things, maybe even at cocktail parties.

There may be further confusion about the job description, and the fact that a woman is doing it. "Aren't ministers people who lead a church, give sermons, and do weddings and funerals? Why call yourself a minister if you're actually an administrator?" Some people may be quite used to women as ministers, others curious about my career choice, and still others affronted, even citing scripture to support their position. Many may wonder why anyone is still practicing such an outdated profession.

And what about the seminary part? The word comes from the Latin *seminarium,* meaning garden, seed plot, nursery, place for cultivation. If the average citizen is even aware that one of these places is in their midst, do they feel that any truly seminal ideas are germinating there? What are its students being educated to do in society and will that matter much?

Presbyterian. Sixty years ago in America, this would have made me part of a vigorous Protestant "mainline." Now we can practically pinpoint the year, fast approaching, in which the denomination could become extinct. It is likely that my questioner knows nothing about the distinctive features of this brand of Protestantism, nor that its representative governance structure was a model for American democracy. (Many Presbyterians, for that matter, no longer know these things.) My questioner may initially be cautious, wondering what brand of Christian I will prove to be — the proselytizing kind or the tolerant kind. Those from other faith traditions — Muslims, Hindus, or Buddhists, for instance — may not even recognize "Presbyterian" as Christian. Here I usually get high marks for actually doing multifaith work and having at least a passing acquaintance with their particular religious tradition or practice.

Finally, "minister" inevitably brings us to the question of "God." Ministers are understood by some as agents or intermediaries for God. But the person to whom I am introducing myself may not feel intermediaries are necessary. Or may be convinced that God is dead, unreachable, or an irrelevant category. If "God" does have meaning for the person, it may not be my meaning. Is God the benevolent bearded ancient in some heaven somewhere? A higher power, an inexpressible spirit? Gendered or not? To be found within nature or in human form? Is the name so powerful that one cannot invoke it? One in three or one among many? Within all of us or an absentee landlord? What images of God, if any, work for both of us? If we were to pursue the conversation, would we be able to talk about our differences?

Most often, when I say I am a minister, people respond with the disclaimer, "I'm not religious." Some may quickly add, "But I'm spiritual." "Spiritual" is a label that is gaining a following, even among those who belong to a church, synagogue, or some other form of organized religious community. For some, "spiritual" means religion-lite, designed to liberate both God and seeker from the trappings of organized religion. This can be handy in times of faith transitions because it seems to allow a person to retain the good and jettison the bad. "Spiritual" speaks to the ongoing hunger to be in relationship to that which is beyond us while freeing us from the rules of how to go about that. It may connote a range of activities we can pursue on our own terms, possibly alone. "Spiritual" seems to encourage religious shopping and experimentation. People feast on a smorgasbord of options, weaving together occasional attendance at high holiday services with bagels and the *New York Times,* Sunday soccer, yoga, meditation, or wilderness adventure. Those for whom traditional religious images and practices still resonate find this spirituality "new age," indiscriminately eclectic, and uncommitted. In some forms, it may well be. But if we grant that in many seekers the phenomenon stems from a genuine hunger, we must ask what soul-satisfying food is missing from our collective religious plate.

Infectious Passion for Doing Justice

I believe people are hungry for ways to bring the whole of themselves to their work in the world, to make meaningful contributions to our life together in ways that honor the cultural diversity that is now so evident. I offer this book as food for that hunger. It celebrates the stories of women who are breaking the decades-long silence of the religious Left by modeling new forms of public leadership grounded in contemporary forms of faith. Some claim affiliation with mainstream religious perspectives; others expressly do not and may describe their motivations more generally as "spiritual." Each has allowed herself to feel the gap between the world as it is and a vision of how it could be, and has devoted herself to making up the difference.

All have sharp critiques of mainstream religion, but most have not given up on it. Although they are practicing new forms of ethical and religious leadership, they see themselves as connected to the traditions. That is, they seek to revivify the root messages about doing justice which lie at the core of traditional religion. They are progressive Christians, Jews, Muslims, and feminist spiritual-eclectics whose convictions about a better way run so deep that they have invented organizations and movements to change the world.

If you have wondered whether one person can still make a difference, read on. You will hear stories of how a vocation often finds you when you least expect it, and the meaning that comes from pursuing it. These women are irreverent, funny, eloquent, and infectiously passionate about their work. Interviewing them carried me across a threshold in my own professional and religious development. Some of these leaders, like Sister Helen Prejean, activist nun and author of *Dead Man Walking,* are well-known; others are less visible. Whether religious professionals or lay persons, all have been moved in unplanned ways to work courageously and creatively on some of the most difficult areas of human need: homelessness, violence and abuse, criminal justice, immigration, disability, and poverty. Here are glimpses of some of their stories:

As a child, *Melodye Feldman* had been attacked for being a Jew. Thirty years later, driving through Denver, she heard a journalist interviewing a young woman over the din of gunfire in the former Yugoslavia. The young woman was about to turn sixteen but felt no desire to continue living with the violence around her. Melodye remembered her own hopes and dreams at that age. In that moment she dedicated her life to working with young people to teach them to make peace. She founded Seeking Common Ground and has been working over a decade with Jewish and Palestinian teenage girls to build peaceful community.

As a child in Korea during the war, *Henna Hahn* had polio, almost died of hunger, and lost her mother to cancer. Years later, she was drawn to a newspaper article about the abused Korean wife of an American GI who had been charged with killing her children. After discovering that the woman had been wrongly accused, Henna worked to have her released to her custody. Henna founded a non-profit called The Rainbow Center to address the complex needs of abused immigrant Asian women.

Because her mother fought for her education, *Riffat Hassan* escaped the oppression of her peers growing up as a young Muslim woman in Pakistan. She became a scholar who specialized in interpreting the Koran from a feminist perspective. Several years ago, women activists on the front line in Muslim countries begged

her to join their desperate fight to stop honor killings — the bru-
tal torture and death of women in Muslim countries by male
members of their own families for purported wrongdoings. She
answered their call by founding an Internet-based international
movement to stop honor killings.

Sister Helen Prejean lived with the illusion that she had been following Jesus faithfully as a nun all of her life until she realized
that she had no direct knowledge of people in need. A chance letter to a man on death row brought her face to face with human
suffering and the criminal justice system. Accompanying him to
his death began the journey that has carried Helen to national
and international prominence as spokesperson in the movement
to fight the death penalty.

These are new ways of being spiritual activists in today's world.
These women's stories need to be heard — not just because they are
doing work in some of the places of greatest need as the caretakers
of our common life — but because they are deeply satisfied doing it.
Instead of being motivated by obligation, they feel joy, passion, and
a deep sense of commitment about their work. All of us at any age
need to hear this as we consider how to meaningfully invest our life
energy. And there may be a larger movement at stake as well, one that
I believe affects the future of the planet.

Breaking the Silence

Because of the convergence of a number of factors, I believe that the
time is ripe for these fresh images of progressive religious leadership to
invigorate both individuals and the broader culture. By "progressive,"
I mean commitment to the values of justice, equity, tolerance, and
pluralism, as well as the ongoing transformation of society to achieve
those ends. I use the term "religious leadership" in the broadest sense

so as to include anyone whose ethical actions in the public arena are grounded in a faith tradition.

My primary concern is the relative silence and invisibility of the religious Left in America, a phenomenon which has had several contributing factors. American religion has been in a state of flux for the last few decades as Judeo-Christian dominance has given way to an appreciation for the broad spectrum of the world's religious perspectives. We now live in a society where mosques rise up in the cornfields of the Midwest, where over a dozen faith traditions are practiced in areas like Suffolk County, Long Island, and where employers across America are pressed to honor a far more diverse variety of religious observances.[1] Some of us are suspicious and threatened by these changes, others challenged and curious, others disoriented or overwhelmed. Whatever our response, religious pluralism is an inescapable reality of American life.

Within the American mainline, a restructuring of the whole religious ecology is under way. Back in the 1940s, the political infrastructure of this country was closely identified with mainline Protestant denominations — Presbyterians, Congregationalists, Methodists, and Episcopalians. Their leaders were the educated elites and "protectors of the Commonweal" whose views on the public good and social issues were regarded as sound public policy. But membership in mainline denominations has been shrinking even as the population has grown, and without a vibrant power base, this form of "social capital" erodes. Further, volatile ideological and theological disputes over such issues as homosexuality and abortion now threaten to overshadow denominational distinctions. Adherents of mainline traditions are beginning to separate out into liberal or conservative, charismatic or evangelical. In this newly evolving ecology, I often find I have more in common with reform Jews than with conservative Presbyterians. It remains to be seen whether this erosion of traditional lines of authority will prove constructive. If new alliances find voice, we may well benefit from a richer articulation of a diversity of views.

Even as the religious landscape has been morphing, economics, business, and science have increasingly become the dominant lenses through which people see and comprehend the world. Corporate America stands at the center of society in a manner reminiscent of the church's role in the Middle Ages — as the dominant authority and organizing force. There is the perception that religion, as we have known it, has not kept pace with advances in knowledge and is not easily applied to the complex daily dilemmas of modern life. As a result, American society is becoming more secular even as it becomes more religiously diverse. Although most Americans still say they believe in God, increasingly they do not express their beliefs by belonging to organized religion.

During this period of flux, progressive forms of religion have not been in the public eye. Rather than risk the appearance of speaking from a narrow, sectarian platform or be associated with fundamentalisms that threaten our survival on the planet, many public servants, scholars, and even religious people have avoided the topic altogether. When it comes to religion, there has been a moratorium on public discourse about issues of ultimate significance. Stephen Carter, an Episcopal layman, novelist, and Constitutional law professor at Yale, asserts that in our secular American society religion is portrayed as a hobby and trivialized, particularly by the media.[2] Religious leaders are viewed as inept, corrupt, dangerous, or simply irrelevant.

Missing Connections, a research study published by Auburn Theological Seminary's Center for the Study of Theological Education, corroborates this trend.[3] After interviewing 250 business and community leaders in four cities around the country about their perceptions of seminaries, religious institutions, and their leaders, the study concludes that all were largely invisible in the public arena. Occasionally a reform Rabbi or African-American clergy person would be cited for public activism, but invariably neither institution nor leader (whether liberal or conservative) was seen as an asset in their communities or beyond, but rather as inwardly focused, preoccupied with taking care of their own. They were not invited to the table where decisions of great consequence to their communities were made.

Taken together, these trends in the decades since the 1960s have conspired to relegate religion to the private sphere and its leaders to the caretaking of dying, domesticated institutions. In short, traditional religion has lost its prophetic edge, its power to inspire us with worthy visions of justice, interdependence, and wholeness. Globalism is corporate America's version of a vision, but for millions it fails the test. There is widespread recognition that essential elements are missing, that conscience, integrity, and compassion need to be restored to public deliberation. There is an enduring hunger for a larger purpose. As the singing group Sweet Honey in the Rock puts it, "We who believe in freedom cannot rest until it comes."[4]

Religious perspectives, reframed by global awareness, still belong at the center of public life. Those who argue that such centrality would violate the separation of church and state subvert the meaning intended by the Founding Fathers. The Constitution's provision was intended to protect us from the potential tyranny of a single religious perspective allied with and supported by our government. It was intended to encourage a vigorous pluralism — to preserve the right of free expression of diverse religious perspectives — not to cleanse the public arena from religious influence. In this era of globalism, concerns about the adequate separation of *business* and state might be much more to the point.

If we are to keep the dark side of both religion and secularism in check, people of mature faith must be encouraged to speak out as they have before. History offers us many examples of leaders who drew upon religious texts, symbolism, and metaphor to build effective social reform movements — Martin Luther King Jr., Reinhold Niebuhr, Dorothy Day, Elizabeth Cady Stanton, and the Grimke sisters, to name a few. Their commentaries about matters of national welfare, civil rights, war, peace, and justice bore weight even with those who disagreed with their theological beliefs. They were those who practiced a resistance faith by critiquing the status quo and working for correctives to abuses of power by government and other institutions, including religious ones. The anti-slavery, anti-segregation, and anti-war movements in this country were all fueled by a religious vision that anticipated equality, human dignity, and freedom. Though feminism is regarded by many as a secular movement, there have always been feminists, myself included, whose activism has been fueled by a powerful Spirit.

Those who would practice a resistance faith in twenty-first-century America have a challenge that earlier reformers did not face. They can no longer assume that Americans share a common religious vocabulary. In an unprecedented way, they will need to call out the deeper currents of Spirit that run through us all — secular humanists, Christians, Jews, Native Americans, Hindus, Muslims, and Buddhists. To do this effectively, they will need fresh images and new language. People's assumptions about religion need to be opened up for reconstruction.

How will this necessary reinterpretation and renewal occur?

We are accustomed to thinking of entrepreneurs in a business context. They are people who have revitalized business in recent decades by acting with vision, courage, and creativity to offer products, services, and sometimes radically new organizational structures in response to an increasingly diverse and complex global marketplace. I consider the women I interviewed to represent a new breed — the spiritual entrepreneur. Their example helps us envision ways to enter this uncharted territory. To join entrepreneurial brilliance with a willingness to address the complexities of human need, to be patient yet restless for change, to exercise compassion and strategic shrewdness, all as an expression of a "whole life" — these are the kinds of worthy commitments for which our culture hungers. The common patterns that emerge from the stories of these women leaders may guide and inspire us at this critical juncture in the evolution of religious tradition and activism.

Beginning to Hear Their Voices

I considered the lives of these modern reformers a rich mystery to be probed, so I spoke at length with each of them. There were questions I asked them all, designed to help me understand what motivated them to respond to injustice and suffering as they have. Often, we began by talking about the organizations they had created — the values embedded in them, the people they were designed to serve, the challenges and satisfactions of running them. I asked how they had come into the work, both in the immediate sense, and over the course of their whole lives. What did they remember from growing up that still affected their actions now? What were the important influences in their lives? How did they sustain themselves over the long haul? Did they struggle with fear or uncertainty? Did faith have anything to do with their public commitments? Given the myriad ways the Divine can be understood, what did God or Spirit look like to them? Did they talk about God with others and if so, how? If not, why not?

I want to take you into one of those interviews now to give you a feel for how one woman speaks to these questions. Each woman's story was different, but I did begin to see some patterns in their responses which I believe are useful clues. Gretchen's story touches upon most of them. By listening to it, we begin to hear what a progressive voice sounds like again.

◆ ◆ ◆

In the mid 1980s, Gretchen Buchenholz, then the forty-year-old executive director of a day care center, set out to do an errand related to her work and "accidentally" walked through a door that changed her life.

I was probably preoccupied, I no longer remember. I was supposed to go into 250 Church Street but instead I walked into 251, and I saw what I saw, which was sickening, shocking. The first thing I saw were little children knocking on a metal door begging for something to drink or eat. . . . There were about seventy-five families there, some on the floor sleeping next to one another. The whole place stank, primarily of diarrhea. There were knuckle marks on the door, but they only went up to the height where little children could reach, and they were begging the people on the other side of the door for food. It was really something that you would be sickened by in the fourth world, but here in New York City, we're talking about a very affluent time, something so foreign. I was really outraged, and at the same time moved to do something about it.

Gretchen's response was instinctive. "I made three phone calls very quickly." One was to the head of disaster relief from the Red Cross whom she knew from volunteer work; the second was to the deputy mayor of operations to request an immediate food delivery; and the third was to the *New York Times* to get a photographer and reporter. She later told me that volunteer work in a soup kitchen had helped her realize the power of the press in focusing public attention and initiating change. No one, she believed, would knowingly perpetuate a situation like this.

Though Gretchen's three phone calls had set larger factions in motion, there was one more move she made that day. It was simple, direct, and personal. "I also went to the neighborhood deli and brought back some big bags of bread and peanut butter and juice even though it wasn't enough for everybody."

Gretchen Buchenholz had never thought of herself as an activist. "I was an innocent bystander. I had no training, gift, talent, knowledge. I had quarters for phone calls." And yet Gretchen also believes that none of us is really an innocent bystander.

When people allow atrocities to occur and they are silent, just as during the Holocaust, the silence is an act. It means you go along with it. Silence is complicity. I don't care what your reason is — you don't throw mothers and babies out of shelters onto the street and then rip the kids away. That's a sin. Whatever our government says, it's a sin. And everyone should be saying that. There has to be a groundswell of protest. This is everyone's responsibility.

Gretchen's way of protesting what she saw that day was to form a non-profit organization — the Association to Benefit Children (ABC) which would begin to "challenge and to change the myriad threats to childhood."[5] Over the years, ABC has developed into a network of programs which advocate for policy reform as well as provide direct services to children and their families.

ABC is a direct reflection of Gretchen's deepest values. When I asked her to explain this linkage, she said:

It's the simplest, most obvious thing, and that is that children are entitled to joy and growth and families and food in their bellies and the opportunity to play and sing and be loved. And a family needs a community, and a community needs the city and the state and government.... It's really very simple — any child anywhere in the world is entitled to a decent place to sleep, a full belly, a loving family, and sometimes shoes.

As a child, Gretchen's own hold on these elements had not always been secure. Her family was very poor and moved often. Her mother, a single parent, had a serious heart condition which sometimes prevented her from working. For a time, she had to place her three children in an orphanage run by nuns. Gretchen remembers her mother as

an incredibly courageous woman who went on and ultimately gathered us back. She visited us every Sunday when she wasn't too ill. And we wanted very badly to get out of there. One time,

I remember she brought me a helium balloon with a cat or a tiger on it. And then she took us to some waterfront like Rye or Pelham for our visit. Well, the balloon got away from me, and I was wailing, and I remember — and this is just a flash — she said, "Don't worry, that balloon is going to" — sorry, this makes me want to cry — "some child in Europe who has nothing." I think that was one of the most formative things in my life — the message that I had plenty to give.

There was also the responsibility to not walk by if you saw something. It was never like a solemn, pious thing, but you couldn't walk by, ever, with anything. That's what I grew up with.

Under Gretchen's leadership, ABC has evolved into a coordinated network of children's organizations. Gretchen directs eight programs in different locations, works on social policy issues at the city and state level, and frequently testifies on children's issues at congressional and senate hearings. Though she has no law degree, she has mastered the legal intricacies of child welfare. Yet when I asked her about the source of her greatest satisfaction, she pointed to the children.

It's not the big stuff and the big accomplishments, though of course that helps. It's the really simple things. Daily things. Seeing a child who didn't have a family go into a family, hearing that laugh outside, first steps. . . . I like having my office in a place where I can always involve myself with the workings of the programs, the staff, with the children, with the families. And I do that many times a day, because that smile is something I need to remember what it's all about. That's the juice I need, that's where I get it.

While we were on the subject of motivational "juice," I asked her how she felt about her work. Did she consider it a passion or a calling, or how would she name it?

None of those words. I really think of it as the grains of sand that build community, the grains of sand that build solutions. I don't think of it as major at this point. It's the tiny role each of us plays in this unimaginably immense galaxy. When I say one grain I mean there's a transcendent something that we all belong to, that we have a shared and mutual responsibility to be respectful and protective and responsive to all things. All things. It's something that I do without thinking because . . . you can't not do it. I don't think of it as a calling or a mission or anything in religious terms like that. I'm not a woman of faith in that sense.

Her answer surprised me. I and others who knew her work considered her a deeply faithful person. She clearly had ethical sensibilities, often spoke like a prophet, and acted with moral courage. Later she told me she had been raised as a Catholic, had taught Sunday School for a time, and still found inspiration in certain passages of Scripture. Yet old notions of what it meant to "be reverent" prevented her from claiming any affiliation now.

I guess I still have the idea that you accept Catholicism whole or not at all, that you're not really able to eat at the table if you don't accept it all. And I'm not ready to do that.

I sensed that Gretchen actually had a form of faith that wasn't held well by current denominational boundaries and dogma. As our conversation continued, she revealed her profound disappointment with religious leaders and institutions that were not using their resources to make a difference in the lives of the needy.

There's a wonderful line in Archibald MacLeish's play, *J.B.* Do you know it? Someone says, "The candles in all the cathedrals are out, all the lights are out, there's nothing but darkness. Blow on the coals of my heart." You know, you think of just that little bit of fire left in a coal and you blow on it, and I feel like I'm doing that. I'm sorry to say that about the churches and synagogues and mosques, but that is how I feel. So much blowing is needed now. Whereas here with the children the light is clear in every face.

When I asked about obstacles to the success of her work, she offered a critique of the entire mainstream ethos — socio-economic, political, and religious.

I think right now the biggest obstacle is the rhetoric from government and the media that portrays the poor as the enemy to be punished, to be hidden, under the guise of saying that they are helping the poor to be less dependent. Soon they're going to be including children in that. The public argument has squeezed out the voices of faith. It has swallowed up and silenced, to a great degree, the impulse we all have to care for the poor, to care for the least of us. All of our traditions tell us that we should do that, and that we're diminished if we don't. Horrible things have happened, horrible things . . . and the church has participated by its silence and inaction.

Despite this sharp critique, she remained hopeful about possibilities for transformation.

The moral dimension has to be put back in or what are we? We're not a civilized people. We've allowed greed and power [to gain ground] — and there's always that potential in a democratic society. But I think that there is also the potential to turn that around, and that's the task at this point. We have a free press, we have the courts, we have the access to advocacy, and I think that we have to do our job. . . . I think we've lost our moral bearings for the time being, but don't think they're lost for good. We just need to trim the sails here. That's the fight. If anything feels like my mission, that's it.

Though I did not want to force the title upon her, this is precisely the kind of faith and progressive religious leadership that I had hoped to bring into view. None of us quite yet knows its contours, but women like Gretchen are helping to define it.

Gretchen was clearly working outside of the usual boxes, or at least at the margins of our reigning paradigms. Given her maverick status and the magnitude of the obstacles, I wondered if she found the work taxing or depressing. Had she ever experienced burnout or wanted to quit?

> It's all in the struggle. You never get to the end because there isn't one. So I don't know what you'd be quitting. Yes, there are tremendous disappointments. But first of all, you're so busy you can't focus on any single one of them for long. There's certainly loss and grief and sorrow, and if you ever come close to it, it's a baby's funeral. But then you leave it, because funerals have that quality of sending you back to celebrate this life by investing in others. If you ever really do feel pretty daunted you have the other guys who depend on you as part of a team. So no. And number one, I have fun every day. The children are funny and beautiful and that makes my work wonderful.

"Is there any way in which it's a sacrifice?" I probed. "Isn't there a huge cost?"

> Not at all. It's a huge gain. I've gotten and gotten and gotten. It's never boring, at any level. There's joy, fun, an opportunity to be creative, to accomplish stuff. I think I'm really lucky. I don't think I ever was without a sense of purpose, I just thought I was going to have a different career. I have a great, great job.

Gretchen called her workspace, which included the children, "holy ground." When we took a tour of one of her buildings after the inter-view and watched the children on the rooftop playground, she pointed to the steeple of the church building that abutted hers and said: "It's good to be in the shadow of the church."

◆ ◆ ◆

In a way, Gretchen's story is a hologram of this book: a single slice capable of revealing the whole portrait of this new breed, the religiously progressive entrepreneur. All of the clues I later recognized as patterns are there.

Like children's knuckle marks on a door. Chapter 2 explores the compelling incidents that drew these women into their work and the nature of the organizations they founded in response. Infusing entrepreneurship with soul gives entirely new meaning to "niche market," "risk assessment," and "success."

Peanut butter. Another key clue. It wasn't Gretchen's entire response, but it was one of the first ones — small and personal. Organizations can and do grow from such simple acts. Chapter 3 reveals how and why these women leaders made a point of keeping such intimate exchanges part of their regular routine, even as their organizations and leadership responsibilities expanded.

A shared and mutual responsibility to be respectful, protective, and responsive to all things. For the most part, these women would not call themselves leaders until they had redefined the term for me. Chapter 4 explores their ambivalence about traditional notions of leadership and the ways they sought to complement them with images embodying relatedness, collaboration, and humility.

Blowing on coals. Gretchen, like others, shied even more from the term "religious leader." Her critiques of institutional religion were among the harshest in the study, yet she still found it "good to be in the shadow of the church." Chapter 5 delves into the complex relationship with religion that these leaders have, and how they are bearers of religion in a double sense: wrestling with its burdensome shadow while carrying forward its valuable core. With new images of God and fresh interpretations of teachings essential to all world religions, these women reveal that though the fire of progressive faith may have been banked in recent decades, it is far from extinguished.

When some of the ordained ministers in the group balked at being called religious leaders, I knew the toll that the silence of the Left had taken. Yet silence is an act. Chapter 6 is devoted to finding voice. Now that so much traditional language has become associated with the Religious Right, liberals and progressives must experiment with fresh ways of conveying spiritual meaning. Doing this successfully in twenty-first-century America involves a multi-lingual skill which these women leaders are just beginning to develop.

Gretchen is not only unafraid to resist the status quo, she "can't not do it." Outrage at knuckle marks carried her into "a great, great job" — a job in which workplace and holy ground are synonymous. Chapter 7 challenges all of us who live compartmentalized lives, splitting ourselves into personal versus professional, private versus public. To a one, these women insisted on living whole, seamless lives in which their actions in the world were in harmony with their deepest beliefs.

How did they have the conviction to do this? Chapter 8 reviews formative influences from each woman's history, trying to answer the question of how their motivation for religious entrepreneurship developed. It turns out it had everything to do with the balloon drifting high into the Pelham sky, carrying its memorable message about loss, need, and the inexhaustible resources of the human heart.

Why do people like Gretchen fascinate us — and give us pause? Perhaps because they remind us of our own latent potential, and what we risk by moving toward it. Perhaps because we sense that the future of the planet may depend on there being more of this type of person. Will there be enough, and will they appear in time?

Religion is a potent, even dangerous force, capable of sponsoring both richer life and unspeakable destruction. It all depends on how we interpret it, how it informs our actions in the world. Pondering the stories of these women leaders has put me into a different relationship with my own power. Chapter 9 includes the story of how these women inspired me to co-found an international, multifaith youth leadership program called Face to Face/Faith to Faith. It also explores more broadly the implications these stories may have for readers of all kinds.

Instead of breaking us apart, our religious traditions may hold the key to our reconnection as they speak to the aching gap between what is and what could be. Holding to such visions gives people the strength to be prophetic, resist the mainstream, overcome obstacles, and move beyond the tragic reality of the moment. Being in relationship to an energy called God, as revealed through many different religious traditions, calls us to live together pursuing justice, mercy, and peace. These are the organizing principles of a moral social fabric. The women in this book, living their seamless lives, lead the way.

Chapter 2

THE TREASURE
IN THE DARK

Touch Me, Be with Me

Rabbi Mychal Springer, now associate dean at Jewish Theological Seminary, was chaplain at New York's Beth Israel hospital at the time of our interview. When I asked her how she felt her work in the hospital affected the broader culture, she said:

> People in society at large ignore pain and suffering, and focus on how good everything is. You know, "I'll tell you my triumphs and you tell me your triumphs." Yet then we're all isolated. My sensibility from the hospital is, "I know that we're hurting and let's make room for that." And that's where community really happens. I did some pulpit work for a few years, part-time, and I would always weave stories from the hospital into my sermons, and people would come up to me and say, you know, I have breast cancer and what you said really resonated with me, or this person in my family has AIDS, or this person's getting divorced or this person has infertility. All the things that really matter to people that nobody asked about because it's this polite society that says we're all shining. Martin Marty talks about how we're great at summertime — all light and no shadow. Well, the minute you say, "Hey, I live in the realm of the shadow, and that's okay," people come crawling out and say, "Touch me, be with me." And it just makes everything different.

23

Rather than being receptive to "the realm of the shadow," increasing numbers of us now use chemistry to help keep darkness at bay. The decade of the 1990s showed a 230 percent increase in the use of antidepressants in the US.[6] Data from various studies indicates that the use of antidepressants among children grew anywhere from three- to tenfold between 1987 and 1996, with a further 50 percent rise in prescriptions between 1998 and 2002.[7] Once considered a medical specialty, mood altering seems to have been mainstreamed. Eighty-five percent of prescriptions are now written by general practitioners; 11.2 percent by psychiatrists.

Is this really an effective strategy for dealing with what ails us, individually and culturally? If we numb ourselves to the suffering of our world, what sort of dwelling place will we bequeath to the next generation and the next?

The Mystery of Matter

The women leaders in this book relied on a different form of chemistry to deal with darkness — the ancient art of alchemy. Since the time of the Greeks and Egyptians, and on into medieval Europe, people fascinated with the mystery of matter sought to transmute base materials into something of great value. Though we sometimes refer to this as "turning lead into gold," alchemical texts actually describe the purpose of the work more broadly as creating "a transcendent, miraculous substance, which is variously symbolized as the Philosophers' Stone, The Elixir of Life, or the universal medicine. The procedure is, first, to find the suitable material, the so-called *prima materia,* and then to subject it to a series of operations that will turn it into the Philosophers's Stone."[8]

The link with our women leaders is the phrase "find the suitable material." If the elixir of life is what one ultimately seeks, where does one begin?

The conundrums and imagery of alchemy have fascinated some prominent world thinkers, including psychoanalyst Carl Jung, who discovered in it striking parallels to the dynamics experienced by individuals undergoing transformation through psychoanalysis. Jung based his therapeutic process on the knowledge that shadow is a necessary complement to light. Each articulates the other. Taken together, they body forth the whole. Given this, the ongoing task of human life is not to avoid the shadow, but to make the counterintuitive move toward it, to recognize and learn to hold in balance the tension of the opposites, light and darkness, without identifying solely with either. For Jung, the elixir of life — the elusive experience of wholeness — was only available to those who, whether through suffering, compassion, courage, or desperation, began the work of *re-collecting* all they had rejected.

> Although of great inward value, the *prima materia* is vile in outer appearance and therefore despised, rejected, and thrown on the dung heap.... Psychologically, this means that the *prima materia* is found in the shadow, that part of the personality that is considered most despicable. Those aspects of ourselves most painful and most humiliating are the very ones to be brought forward and worked on.[9]

As the client embraces this material, the therapeutic process heats up, becoming charged with emotion and struggle. Alchemy texts are filled with references to the *vas* or retort in which the *opus* unfolds. It must be a closed vessel, able to withstand intense heat, designed to hold whatever interim forms of matter arise on the way to transmutation. Eventually, a new substance emerges — in therapy, a new perspective which sees both light and dark, and can embrace a larger and more complex whole. It takes courage and patience to turn toward the darkness, toward what looks like base metal or dross, but only in so doing is true life found. That is the paradox.

I suggest that people who notice and take on suffering and oppression in our society are working on behalf of the wholeness of our collective life together. I like to think of the women leaders whose stories we are following as social alchemists because they recognize the starting point, "the suitable material," for our collective healing. They notice the rejected ones of our society — those people whom others would avoid or discard, the social issues that seem unsolvable — and are able to see what others cannot: the human potential or gold within, the possibilities for transformation. Instead of walking by or wishing them away, they act on the conviction that these people are the children of God capable of thriving. As we will see, their organizations are like so many alchemical retorts, working a mystery in our midst.

Jung knew why the alchemists of old kept at it: the dark mass of matter they sought to transmute was actually themselves. The elixir — the secret of life — is to manifest wholeness, within and between us. A modern-day social alchemist would say that the mystery of matter is better understood if we ask ourselves "what is the matter?" and "what finally matters?" As a society, what is the matter with us, and what are our ultimate values? Start where the suffering is and boil it down to essence. The answer lies within the matter itself — in *mater* Herself. As these women's lifework shows, transmutation occurs when the rejected cornerstone of *mater* (the feminine) is brought to bear on public issues.

Ancient alchemy belongs to a time when science and religion were still joined. "A prominent feature of the *opus* is that it is considered a sacred work requiring a religious attitude."[10] As ensuing chapters will show, the women leaders practice their modern-day alchemy in a way that I feel appropriately rejoins the sacred and secular in pursuit of societal wholeness.

Social Alchemists at Work

Embracing the Untouchables

We usually associate entrepreneurship with the business world. The women you will meet in this book are social and spiritual entrepreneurs because they have invented organizations designed to influence the dynamics of how we live together. When I spoke with them, over half were executives of organizations they founded while others held major positions in existing ones or were spokespersons for national or international causes. Almost all worked with the disenfranchised and discarded — people in broken environments, the homeless, battered women and children, AIDS sufferers, women prisoners and ex-convicts, people on Death Row, persons with disabilities, and those in crisis.

Laura Jervis, founder of West Side Federation for Senior Housing, which provides over a thousand units of low-income housing for the elderly poor and those with special needs on New York City's Upper West Side, told me of her organization's commitment to taking risks on behalf of the marginalized:

> I think that we are more willing and able to take risks where other people are not. I mean, we will house people that nobody else will touch.... [She goes on to describe a case where they took in a pedophile who was developmentally disabled and mentally ill.] These are people who really nobody else would house or tolerate. And our staff does it with a full heart.

Jan Orr-Harter, formerly pastor of Jan Hus Presbyterian Church on Manhattan's tony East Side, expressed a similar resolve to reach out to young adults, homeless people, people in recovery from addiction, gays and lesbians, activists, and people other churches just did not want.

So, it was a kind of strange constellation of people that we would set out to look for. . . . We decided that somebody needed to be the down-and-dirty, scrappy church of the neighborhood and work on more difficult issues, and that's what we were called to do. That's who we set out to find.

Other women leaders designed their organizations as incubators for new and alternative social values. Barbara Dobkin founded Ma'yan, the Jewish Women's Project, in part to nurture women's leadership and serve as a seedbed for feminist values in the wider Jewish community. Melodye Feldman created a feminist model of peace education focused on young women from Israeli and Palestinian communities.

Their work covers the gamut from direct services for immediate needs to advocacy and education designed to provoke systemic change. Direct services include providing food, shelter, job training, and legal services. Education ranges from English language classes for clients to education of the public around social issues like the criminal justice system, violence against women and children, or the death penalty. Advocacy takes the form of filing legal suits against city or state agencies involved in warehousing babies in their care or lobbying elected officials to change policy on a constellation of neighborhood issues like poverty, drug abuse, and crime.

Building the Vessel: Creating Holding Environments

Whether within organizations of their own design or in established institutions, these women are doing the alchemical work of transformation, seeking to change individual lives, communities, points of view, and unjust dynamics within social systems. As I listened to how they used their organizations to do so, I found a spatial image repeating itself in my mind's eye — "holding environment." Although I first heard the term in a seminary class on depth psychology and theology over twenty years ago, it remains for me a most evocative image. It refers to an hospitable space created to provide physical and psychological safety mixed with appropriate challenge and structure so as to best sponsor wholeness and healing. Such an environment offers the opportunity for dependence and independence, for intimacy and separation, for optimal growth and fullness of life. The term was coined by British child psychiatrist Donald Winnicott[11] to describe how the relationship between psychiatrist and client could mirror the intimate bond between mother and child. This, he felt, offered an optimal environment within which a child or client could move through the developmental stages necessary for maturation or healing. It struck me that some of these women's organizations were offering their clients precisely this form of relationship.

The term "holding environment" has found its way into the work of others who are thinking about the kind of leadership needed to meet today's challenges. Harvard leadership theorist Ronald Heifetz is one of these. He uses the term more broadly to describe how leaders can facilitate group work on the especially difficult issues he calls adaptive challenges — problems for which leader and group alike have no known "fix." In this context, a holding environment is:

> . . . any relationship in which one party has the power to hold the attention of another party and facilitate adaptive work. I apply it to any relationship which has a developmental task or opportunity including the relationships between politicians and their nations, nations and other nations, coaches and their teams, managers and subordinates, and even relationships between friends. The holding environment can generate adaptive work because it contains and regulates the stresses that work generates.[12]

Heifetz says that adaptive leaders provide an environment that holds the participants while they work with complex issues, clarify their values, make appropriate adaptations, and envision new directions. The purpose of adaptive leadership is to bring the reality of "what is" into better alignment with a vision of "what could be."

The image of the holding environment is useful for thinking about the contexts and dynamics that sponsor change. In my work at Auburn, we draw on the seminary's role as convener and catalyst to bring together figures from diverse worlds — business, academia, religion, and politics — in hopes of generating new energies and focus around intractable issues like the Israeli-Palestinian conflict. A key ingredient in this work is creating time set apart from daily duties, time reserved and protected expressly for the purpose of envisioning new patterns of thought and action. Groups like this sometimes gather in a room that has a recessed well in the middle of it — an architecture which literally seems to hold and gather our thoughts. The leader's role in such convocations is not to offer answers but rather to help keep all participants creatively engaged with the most difficult questions.

The holding environments which the women leaders have designed serve as the vessel or locus for change. Some emphasize direct services, providing hospitable space, both physical and psychological, that help clients, staff, and even the leaders themselves to thrive. Laura Jervis thinks of this as functioning like the best of families.

> For so many people we are their family, and [there is] this sort of joke about how we're a full service operation — that we marry, bury, everything. That's really true. I mean, we are there for people in a way that only the best of families are.

Other leaders have created spaces where attention can be focused around public policy issues. The emphasis here is more on advocacy and education to effect systemic solutions to difficult social problems like violence against women. Most of the organizations function in a hybrid way, working on specific public problems through multiple approaches — direct services, research, education, advocacy, and policy reform.

Regardless of the specific dynamics, this work of transformation takes place in spaces set apart from the wider milieu wherein new insights and behaviors can be modeled and incubated, where alternatives to mainstream culture can be envisioned and practiced. If mainstream solutions leave a vacuum, these women leaders seek to fill the gap. In this way, the holding environments they have created function as vessels of resistance that complement or correct (and in so doing, critique) mainstream practices by modeling a better way. These women are not merely duplicating services; they are inventing those which the social safety net seems unable or unwilling to provide. Often, this means upholding more fully the values to which mainstream culture may give lip service but nevertheless does not enact.

Who would not agree, when asked directly, that "childhood is a terrible thing to waste" or that "every child needs food, shelter, education and love"? Yet there is often a gap between our ideals and our actions. Remember how Gretchen Buchenholz came upon a holding pen in New York City for homeless families in which hungry children were clawing on a metal door begging for food? Her creation of the Association to Benefit Children was simultaneously a critique of an egregious breach of a social contract and a viable alternative, embodying the values of shelter, safety, love, and education that society had overlooked. As a vessel of resistance that actually incarnates societal ideals, it now serves as a conscience embedded within the larger body politic, calling it to account for its shortcomings. Holding environments like Gretchen's are hospitable places were people are treated with dignity, women are empowered, the disabled, poor and suffering are helped toward a greater sense of wholeness, and insights are crystallized about how to make whole social systems more just and inclusive.

I asked each of the women leaders about the internal workings of their holding environments, hoping to better understand how their ethics and vision played out organizationally. I found that these women place a high value on integrity — within themselves, and for their organizations. It is important to them that their staffs experience the same quality of hospitality and sponsorship as their clients do, and that their organizations function internally according to the same values of inclusiveness, compassion, and interdependent relationship that they model toward clients. As such, their organizations become microcosmic examples of a society operating under a new set of rules. As difficult as these acts of incarnation can be, that is what these women leaders seek to do, often with great success. Henna Hahn's story is just one example of what a holding environment can be.

Offering the Promise of the Rainbow

In the mid 1990s, in a borough of Manhattan, Henna Hahn, a Methodist minister, founded the Rainbow Center, a shelter for Korean women who have been abused by their American GI husbands or other men. She named it after the rainbow that appears in the biblical story of Noah as a sign of God's covenant or promise with the people that the world will not be destroyed by flood again. In speaking of the women served by her organization, Henna said that they, too, need such a promise: "They need the rainbow — no more punishment."

Henna would probably tell you that a woman named Chong Sun France was the true founder of the Rainbow Center. In 1992, when Henna was working in a church supporting the specific needs of Korean women in international marriages, a colleague sent her a clipping from a newspaper. It reported the story of a woman named Chong Sun France who for six years had been imprisoned in North Carolina for the second-degree murder of her child. Henna responded by going to visit the woman in jail. Hearing her story, she realized that she had been falsely accused. Chong France, who spoke no English, had fled from her abusive American GI husband with her two small children. She began working nights in a bar, leaving her children to sleep in a motel room. One evening the two-year-old had tried to play with the TV, pulled it over on top of himself, and was killed. The police took her grief-stricken words, "I killed my son," as a confession.

Henna began a year-long campaign to free her. Through her efforts, Chong France's sentence was commuted; she was granted parole and placed in Henna's custody. As Henna explained, the Rainbow Center was founded out of this encounter. "Who is the owner of this house? Chong France, not me." It would take three years to become a an official 501(c)3 reality, but by 1995 the Rainbow Center became the first Korean women's shelter in the United States and continues to be a model.

Today, the Rainbow Center is a not-for-profit organization that provides a full range of services to women who experience bi-cultural and bi-racial challenges. Direct services include food and shelter, counseling, networking with social service providers, English and citizenship classes, and legal assistance. The Center also gets involved in advocacy campaigns on human rights issues. For example, they intervened on behalf of a Korean woman, a prostitute with AIDS, who faced deportation because of her illegal status in this country.

In addition to these essential tangible services, Rainbow Center provides much more as a holding environment for outcast Korean women in crisis. Henna, like Laura Jervis, thinks of her organization as being like the best of families. She has modeled it on the Korean cultural concept of *Chin-Jeong Jip,* which translates as "a mother's house." In Korean tradition, when a woman marries, she goes to her husband's home, where she assumes a servant role for her husband's family. However, there are certain circumstances in which she may return to her mother's house, as, for example, for a family wedding or when she experiences morning sickness during pregnancy. Having a living mother with a house gives a woman status in her husband's home because she always has a place to which she can return. "As a place of refuge, it provides familiarity, physical and psychological safety, care and support from her family, her mother, and the resources of renewal and healing."[13]

The Rainbow Center is a representation of *Chin-Jeong Jip*, the mother's house to which these abused Korean women can "return" to find safety and shelter. Not coincidentally, Henna's own mother died of cancer during the Korean War and she herself suffered from polio and almost died of starvation. Her self-concept for many years thereafter was that of a "poor, motherless child." She began to reexamine this notion as a young adult while taking a class from a feminist theologian who offered her images of God as a source of feminine strength and transforming nurture. Eventually, she told me, through the grace of good therapy, she reconnected with her own mother's version of the same.

> My mother prepared special food, homemade noodles, for the elderly people, and then invited them in. It's very simple and special, healthy food for them. So she made all this for 10 or 15 women. Old ladies, grandmothers, came into my small living room. And then my mother read a book in a loud voice, all night. So these Korean ladies, grandmas, sometimes were crying because the story of the book. This was when I was a small child sleeping. I heard this noise and woke up to see the grandmas' tears, the crying and talking, and then my mother louder and louder. My mother did these kind of things. She was a very unusual woman in all the villages. So that is in my consciousness. After therapy, I realized my mother did all this. Now I do my mother's footsteps, follow her.

Here we see the intimate intertwining of the founder's story with her organization's characteristics. Henna, like the clients she was serving, needed a mother's house to shelter her, and she knew from her own experiences of healing which elements would be most effective.

Feminine imagery is prevalent at the Center. Henna said, "When I opened the Rainbow Center everybody told me, 'You are the mother of the Rainbow Center.' Not! 'So, who is mother?' God! God is mother. God is the mother and we are all the sisters. So, I'm like a big sister." Not coincidentally, Henna's own family of origin included three sisters. "Three sisters is very good supporting and good caring, and good family. That's why I organized this sisters' house."

She explained that many of the women who come to the Center have been drug addicts or prostitutes; many suffer from mental illness. The articulated purpose of the Center is healing, which Henna described as helping to make the women whole and functioning. Judith Herman in her book, *Trauma and Recovery,* asserts that recovery for victims of abuse and trauma occurs in several stages: the establishment of safety, remembrance and mourning, and reconnection with ordinary life.[14] Rainbow Center provides a place for these stages to occur.

Henna estimates that 30 percent of an individual's healing occurs through exposure to "home," such as reconnecting with Korean culture, food, and language; 40 percent through medical or therapeutic intervention; and the remaining 30 percent through religion. She emphasizes that religious healing is not sectarian and does not necessarily involve religious conversion. "My intention is not to make a woman Christian; my only intention is to make her a whole human being who God created originally."

As in strong families, the sharing of familiar food is an important healing ritual at the Rainbow Center. This corresponds to the Korean concept of *ba-sang gong dong che,* translated as "community around a table." This ritual of food and community is reminiscent of a communion motif in a Christian context or a Seder meal in a Jewish one. Henna explained the significance of this shared meal by reciting a poem: "Nobody owns heaven by themselves; everybody shares heaven. Everybody has to share the rice, because the rice is heaven." Thus, food nurtures several dimensions at once. It is physical sustenance, connection to Korean culture and to other sisters, and a medium for touching the spiritual dimension of life.

As the sisters begin to heal and are able to function as human beings again, they are encouraged to become agents of healing themselves. A group of them who call themselves the Dandelion Mission (because of the beauty and hardiness of dandelions in the face of adversity) go out into the streets to seek other homeless and lost Korean women. These sisters of the Rainbow Center are not only the recipients of healing but, like dandelion fluff carried on the wind to spawn new plants, they are empowered to be agents in the transformation of others. Developing such a sense of agency and capacity in its clients is an expressed goal of the Center.

The nature of the hospitality at The Rainbow Center is multifaceted, extending beyond the basics of shelter and food to include social services, education, companionship, and reaching out to others. The insights of Dr. Mindy Fullilove, one of the women I interviewed for this book, are helpful here. She is a research psychiatrist whose work focuses on people at risk in poor communities. She explores the intimate relationship of human beings to their environments and concludes that they basically need four ingredients to thrive: hearth, heart, grail, and soul.[15]

Fullilove's quaternity captures the essence of how the Rainbow Center functions as a holding environment. It offers a place for sisters to satisfy their basic strivings for a home, a safe place with good food (*hearth*); loved ones, people with whom one can develop trusting relationships (*heart*); work that has meaning, first in the form of reaching out through the Dandelion Mission and eventually through jobs (*grail*); and finally a spiritual life, a connection to God, not in a sectarian sense but as that which fosters wholeness (*soul*). The Rainbow Center functions as an alchemical vessel transforming the lives of the sisters and, through advocacy work on immigration issues, the policies that shape systems at the broader societal level.

A Profile of Progressive Public Leadership

There is a private story that links each of the other women in this book to her public commitments and to the nature of the organization she chose to create. Each story is distinct, but taken together, they reveal the kind of ethical stance which I believe gives rise to progressive public leadership grounded in faith. As the book unfolds, we will see how these values and attributes, interwoven, stand behind everything these women do.

Ethic of relationship

emphasizes hospitality, nurturing, and interdependent connection;

understands justice as right relationship.

Ethic of inclusiveness

values diversity and pluralism, especially including those persons whom society might wish to ignore or reject;

prefers collaborative process.

Belief in the possibility of transformation

practices an alchemical understanding of darkness, embracing the rejected cornerstone as a starting place for healing;

works along a personal/systemic continuum, believing that individuals and systems alike can change;

trusts and emphasizes grassroots process.

Entrepreneurial spirit

feels a sense of agency — convinced that one's actions make a difference in the world;

chooses to take risks and work creatively at the margins of social structures, offering fresh patterns of thinking and behavior.

Ethic of seamlessness

bridges realms often kept separate, such as public/private, sacred/secular;

emphasizes integrity — the coherence between belief and practice in both self and organization;

enjoys a sense of vocation — the feeling that one's work sponsors wholeness for both self and world.

Resistance faith

called to alleviate suffering, oppression, and injustice;

feels responsibility to resist evil, not simply avoid it;

serves as a conscience in the body politic, critiquing mainstream values and structures;

relies on inner authority, not necessarily the values mediated by the external authorities, either ecclesial or secular;

reclaims radical/root understandings of religious teachings.

Many of these are evident in the story of Henna Hahn's Rainbow Center. Clearly, the Center is grounded in compassion, inclusiveness, hospitality, and relationship. It was Henna's ability to identify with the plight of these sisters that engendered her passion to found the organization. Her stated mission of "no more punishment," just support for regaining a sense of wholeness, is reflected in the Center's emphasis on fulfilling the basic strivings for hearth, heart, grail, and soul.

This coherence between word and action — between values and day-to-day behavior — is one aspect of what I more broadly call an ethic of seamlessness: the conviction that everything is connected. Another aspect — the bridging of realms often kept separate — may be seen here in Henna's open introduction of spiritual values and language into a secular non-profit addressing a public problem. While it is her conviction that complete healing involves God, she is careful to respect the myriad ways in which this dynamic may be understood.

Henna's work reflects her fundamental belief in the possibility of transformation — that lives can be redeemed and changed. All of her energies are focused on the dynamics of moving the sisters from being victims and social outcasts toward "the whole human beings God created them to be." Recognizing that complete healing means that both people and systems need to change, she has built up a repertoire of interventions which range from direct services to advocacy and policy initiatives.

In typical grassroots fashion, Henna started small by reaching out to one woman in need, Chong France, whose plight came to her attention. Over time, the organization grew, with clients becoming part of the system of outreach to others in need. Throughout it all, Henna, despite her own history of brokenness, evidenced a powerful sense of personal agency, a feeling that this particular work of transformation was not too overwhelming a task. She soon found her agency multiplied. Like hardy dandelion seed, the transformative energy took root in the sisters around her and began spreading farther afield.

Henna is an entrepreneurial risk-taker who knew nothing of 501(c)3 law but taught herself whatever was necessary to start a non-profit organization so as to care for Chong France and the many others like her. Personally and professionally, she has borne the risks and created the funding strategies that keep the doors open.

With no external guarantees or particular encouragement, Henna launched The Rainbow Center out of a deep sense of knowing she was doing the right thing. Something inside drove her to do it and has sustained her over time. Frederick Buechner, Presbyterian minister, beloved preacher, and novelist, speaks of vocation as "the place where your deep gladness and the world's deep hunger meet."[16] It is evident that Henna has found this place in a way of working that is simultaneously a giving and a receiving. Responding to these sisters in need, she finds that her own soul is also fed.

Mothering an Ailing Society

The Rainbow Center is a prototypical holding environment. Several of the women I talked to had similar organizations offering marginalized people the hospitable space and challenge necessary for healthy growth. At the Association to Benefit Children, Gretchen Buchenholz offers food, shelter, safety, fun, and education to enact her conviction that everyone deserves a happy childhood — something she sometimes lacked as a child. Laura Jervis' residences provide a homelike atmosphere in which elderly and mentally ill residents can live and work with dignity and respect.

Other women leaders have introduced an increased level of nurture into existing spaces. Mychal Springer altered the pastoral care program in a large urban hospital to create the awareness that patients and staff alike have spiritual as well as physical needs. Ganga Stone offered nourishing food, companionship, and spiritual support to homebound victims of AIDS who could not feed themselves. Helen Prejean's intensive work accompanying and advocating for prisoners on Death Row introduced into a prison setting alternative values based on the intrinsic worth of every human being as a child of God.

We sometimes hear the critique that such efforts are too limited a response in the face of the pervasive social injustices they seek to address. Detractors argue that such direct services reach relatively few people — perhaps a few thousand at most. Might not time and money be better spent lobbying for public policy changes on a massive scale?

I will return to this question in the next chapter. Here, let me say that I believe these women's organizations already represent a significant shift in that they are one means of introducing into the public sphere traditional feminine values associated with sponsoring healthy growth. By reconstituting the dynamics of the mother-child dyad in the behavior of public organizations, these women leaders are helping to bring feminine wisdom to bear on difficult public issues. Their organizations and approaches may have an important therapeutic effect at the systemic level, mothering an ailing society toward greater wholeness and a more complete justice.

A Commitment to Inclusiveness

A more complete justice requires that no one be excluded. Again we have a question of scope. How far does our hospitality extend? While equality and respect for diversity are American values supported by law, the reality is that many communities, schools, businesses, and houses of worship remain extraordinarily divided by color, culture, ethnicity, class, and religion. By contrast, the genuinely hospitable spaces these women have created for the marginalized demonstrate their deep commitment to inclusiveness. These women leaders build in diversity, not because of legal fiat or out of political correctness, but because of a particular vision of interdependence and connectedness — a conviction that this is the way life should be. Part of their work as alchemists is to broker relationships across barriers that customarily divide us. This is another sense in which their organizations function as vessels of resistance, modeling alternatives to mainstream practices.

These women leaders are particularly sensitive to the injustices of a society like ours which tolerates the marginalization of whole classes of people. Perhaps this is not surprising, given the values of the socially progressive professional circles in which these leaders operate. More striking, however, is the coherence between these professed values and their actual institutions and work. Their organizations are laboratories for tapping the strengths of diverse perspectives and bridging boundaries to bring people together around a common focus.

Connie Baugh's story is a good example. In the span of twenty years, she founded two non-profit organizations that address the needs of women in prison and their children, and founded a church to minister specifically to the needs of ex-prisoners and their families. These organizations offer a combination of direct services and policy initiatives.

While attending seminary, Connie began working with women prisoners at Rikers Island and was confronted with the magnitude of need in the area of legal advocacy. After graduation in 1978, she founded CAFJ, Citizen Advocates for Justice, and built it from the ground up. It offered a range of services for women while they were in prison and after they came out. There was a bail fund for pre-trial detained women and adolescents. Inside-Out-One-on-One connected trained citizen volunteers from the outside to women in prison. It became a model for effectively crossing boundaries of class and race. Connie created some of the first alternatives to jail programs in New York City where women who were non-violent first offenders could do community work instead of jail time.

One of the biggest barriers ex-prisoners face is the feeling of being a social outcast. Connie told me that the women ex-prisoners finally convinced her that what they needed most was a supportive community where they could feel included when they were released from prison:

> When I sat down and really listened to what the women wanted — the kind of community, the feeling that their children were accepted as children of God and were not outsiders, the abuse they took from male clergy, who called them whores and wouldn't baptize their babies because they were not married — I just said, this exclusion cannot continue in the church.

Connie responded by founding a new church for prisoners, ex-prisoners, their family members, and people who felt called to be in ministry with the poor. The Church of Gethsemane was sponsored by the Presbyterian Church (U.S.A.), the denomination to which Connie belonged — but not without a fight. Connie explained to me that, for some, her vision posed a threat on a number of levels.

> One, I was the first woman to organize a Presbyterian Church in New York City, and possibly the nation. There was also the dynamic that I was working with the poorest of the poor, and I was demanding that they be accepted as full brothers and sisters in the faith in the pews, rather than be recipients of charity outside the church walls. Furthermore, the very idea of building a church of the poor that could never be self-sustaining through its own offerings seemed absurd and threatening. And, lastly, the dynamic that I was going to be ordaining ex-felons to be elders, leaders in the Presbyterian Church, giving them a voice in all Presbytery matters.

The inclusion of ex-prisoners as leaders within the church proved a stumbling block for some church authorities. Yet it was essential to Connie's vision. Like Henna Hahn, who involved her client-sisters in the Dandelion Mission to reach others, and like Laura Jervis, who involved client-residents in the running of her buildings, Connie felt that ex-prisoners had to be full participants in the life and decision-making of their church.

The successor to CAFJ, Justice Works Community, a national organization dedicated to criminal justice and policy reform, carries the ethic of inclusiveness further. From the beginning, it was designed as an interfaith organization, although it remained connected to the Church of Gethsemane through its by-laws. Connie explained that "the board would have interfaith representation and support national interfaith efforts. We have a commitment to keeping the board diverse, in terms of race, class and religion. . . . I think we're building a strong interfaith model here for doing justice."

The other women leaders also actively cultivated diversity in their organizations. For example, Mychal Springer helped to make the hospital setting where she supervised pastoral care more hospitable to diverse constituencies by founding a gospel choir that brought together people across lines of religious difference — Jews, Christians, conservatives, black and white. Explaining this innovation, she noted that many of the staff at the lower levels were racial minorities who practiced a "Bible-thumping" Christianity. Within the hierarchy of a Jewish hospital, they had reason to wonder if they counted. As Mychal explained, the gospel choir became a microcosm that usefully redressed the balance.

> One of the reasons that the choir developed the way it did is because the disenfranchised people whose voices aren't heard were given a chance to be in this and to lead with their religion, which is their strength. And since it's a Jewish hospital, the rabbi had to bless it, which she did. It was sheer delight.

The issue of diversity and inclusiveness came up over and over again from all of the leaders I interviewed. Instead of managing diversity as a necessary evil, they trust and cultivate inclusiveness as a means of strengthening their organizations. This commitment distinguishes these women as religious leaders from those traditional leaders who remain focused on sectarian agendas or isolated populations. Mychal, the rabbi, is as concerned that conservative Christians have a voice and a sense of belonging in the Jewish hospital as she is her own kind. These are leaders concerned about a broad public agenda for inclusiveness.

This discovery is particularly noteworthy because it differentiates the women in this book from women leaders in other historical periods — women reformers in the nineteenth century, for example, who were acting in a predominantly white Christian context. The women here have come from a particular religious orientation, but their work takes place in a public arena that is racially, culturally, and religiously diverse. In our modern era, the role of religious leaders committed to progressive social change is more complex. The commitment to inclusiveness that these women leaders exhibit, and the specific leadership competencies they are developing around it, prefigure a style that others will need to adopt to meet today's challenges.

Chapter 3

EVERY PERSON
IS A UNIVERSE

What counts as "making a difference?" Is it enough to help individual people? How many is enough? Even if we ease the suffering of thousands one by one, will this address the roots of the problem? What about the larger context of people's lives — everything from family dynamics, to community values and norms, to the socio-political policies and systems that so profoundly shape us all? Often, these seem such a given that it does not occur to us to question them. Or, even if we understand well their pervasive influence, we doubt our power to shape and transform them. If "the system" seems to be part of the problem, how can anyone begin to "fix" it, especially when "the system" is not a single self-contained thing, but rather a vast web of overlapping, interrelated dynamics? Where do you start? What sorts of interventions might be effective? How can you tell? Will what you choose to do "show" enough to persuade others to help?

I face these questions first-hand in my work with Face to Face/Faith to Faith, the international multifaith youth leadership program I co-founded several years ago. A program designed to shape the lives of fifty teenagers at a time, or even several hundred, seems insignificant to some. I spend a great deal of time fundraising, as do many of the leaders I interviewed. Potential donors, especially men, want "results" — defined as large-scale impact. As one put it to me, "If you could correlate the reduction of suicide bombers to the influence of your program on building peaceful communities, you'd have something there." I co-founded this program because I have every confidence that this correlation exists and will grow. It is no coincidence that I share this confidence with many of the women I spoke with, for it was their philosophy of social change which activated my own.

Discovering the Dance

These women leaders view individuals and systems as a continuum rather than as distinct, separate spheres. Keenly aware of questions of impact and the pressure to adjudicate between the micro and macro, each has found her own way to apply leverage. Partway through my interviews with them, I was surprised to see a pattern taking shape. Many of these women do not choose between individuals and systems. Instead, they seek to make change by moving back and forth between them — so much so, that it seems like a dance step. I call it the one-on-one systemic dance. They alluded to this pattern over and over again without my prompting, and it seemed so related to their satisfaction with their work that I began to take particular note. Even when their organizations grew in scale and scope, the women prized intimate one-on-one work with individuals. What was this about?

Compelled to Take the First Steps

One third of the women identified a single compelling one-on-one encounter as the genesis of their organization. Recall that Gretchen Buchenholz stepped into the wrong building and came upon children clawing at a door for food. That was enough to set her on a different path. Ganga Stone realized that the man dying of AIDS to whom she delivered a bag of groceries had no way of preparing them — and thus unfolded the founding of God's Love We Deliver, a system by which thousands of homebound persons receive nourishing prepared meals each day. It was enough for Henna Hahn to read the story of a woman wrongly convicted of the murder of her children to found the Rainbow Center to deal with the needs of disempowered Asian women. For Ginny Thornburgh, her disabled son's rejection by a church community decades ago ignited an ongoing passion to make religious and other institutions accessible for the disabled. Linda Tarry-Chard had a cup of coffee one day with Helen Lieberman and heard a story of need that she could not ignore. She ended up coordinating an effort to send fifteen thousand Black dolls to South Africa because it was not possible to buy one there after apartheid. Melodye Feldman heard the plight of one teenage girl on a radio show and vowed to connect teenagers to their own power to make a more peaceful world. Over and over again I heard how a passion for justice on a broader scale was awakened in the intimacy of a one-on-one encounter.

Each of these women was involved in related work prior to her encounter: running a day care center, doing hospice work with dying people, focusing on the needs of immigrant Asian women, caring for a disabled child, bridging differences through diversity training, working with youth in camp settings. Yet none had long-range plans which anticipated the new direction. The encounters reoriented them toward largely unmapped territory. The women's first steps into it were intimate, modest acts between one human being and another — buying peanut butter, delivering a bag of groceries, researching a newspaper story, making a space for a son, conversing with a stranger at the request of a friend, committing herself to peace education of youth after hearing the voice of one teenage girl over the din of gunfire. Over time, these acts connected them to a nexus of public issues — such as child welfare, AIDS, disability, violence against women, and economic development — and called forth a broader response. With little or no formal preparation for such undertakings, all six went on to found organizations to respond to the need that the catalytic encounter had crystallized.

Though the remaining women did not identify catalytic encounters immediately preceding the birth of their organizations, many mentioned them as stepping stones in a more gradual evolution toward their current focus. Whether it was watching a parent metamorphosize during the 1960s, or identifying with the story of a prison inmate during an internship in college, or feeling the joy of being trusted by an elderly client during a first excursion as a young social worker, each of these women could identify transforming one-on-one moments that had seeded their current commitments.

An Essential Spiritual Dynamic

The power of these one-on-one encounters seems to be the way the particular and the universal intermingle in them. It is as if the one-on-one encounter is a hologram of a larger story — a microcosmic fragment that reveals the whole. By participating in it, one is already experiencing the dynamics of the larger story. Sensing the macro within the micro, one is already doing the dance. And it is that taste which propels one into ever larger circles.

Sister Helen Prejean was particularly articulate about these dynamics. Her book, *Dead Man Walking*, became the award-winning film with Susan Sarandon playing Sister Helen. She had been a nun for many years but her life took a turn when, at the request of a friend, she began writing to a man on Death Row. She ended up accompanying him to his death as his spiritual advisor. That work with Patrick Sonnier grew into a national movement to end the death penalty in this country. Now over a decade later, she continues her spiritual work with individuals on Death Row, as well as with families of murder victims. When I interviewed her she still prayed regularly with the father of one of Sonnier's teenage victims. Yet she also moves in much wider circles. Through public speaking, writing, and networking, nationally and internationally, she attempts to change the prevailing consciousness on criminal justice issues. The primary purpose of all of her work has been to abolish the death penalty by changing hearts, minds, and public policy. For her, the starting point and ongoing touchstone is the one-on-one exchange:

> Visiting with people on Death Row, to me, is the anchor. That's the baseline. Being with murder victims' families and praying with them and being with people on Death Row — that's the personal. And every person is a universe. My speaking comes out of those experiences, and I think that's why the speaking thing has been so good.... If I didn't maintain personal experiences with people, I would drift out of it, or I'd start putting gloves on and I'd be removed from it. You know, solidarity with poor people and being in their company, and being involved with people who are suffering is an essential spiritual dynamic. Without that you begin to drift away, and you begin to do these commentaries on your experiences — once removed, twice removed, three times removed. So, the presence of people suffering is just essential.

Sister Prejean identifies the intimate one-on-one work — staying close to suffering — as an essential spiritual dynamic, a touchstone that keeps the systemic work alive and connected to reality. Many might find such a move counterintuitive — beyond even the demands of the spiritual disciplines of prayer or meditation. Consider how difficult it is for most of us to visit someone sick or dying in a hospital. What must it feel like to take on the boundless, tangled grief of a prison setting? Startlingly, Sister Helen experienced it as being given a jolt of energy.

> Visiting Patrick, it was just like something happened in my soul after that first meeting. I was hooked for life. There was no way I was going to turn away from this man that I had met. And I just ratcheted along and watched him be executed in front of my eyes. You know, it either paralyzes you or galvanizes you when

you witness something like that. And it had that effect on me. It was like another Baptism. I had a mission.

This mission, she was quick to underscore, needed to engage the wider universe of injustice as well as the individual people most directly affected. All along the continuum, she needed to go about the work of "resisting evil."

If I get in a personal ministry to people on Death Row and then I didn't engage in any of the efforts to change the system of it — to abolish the death penalty — I would be doing something *charitable* — accompanying people to their deaths and comforting them — but I wouldn't be doing anything to resist the evil, and I couldn't do that.

She explained that she had become aware of this distinction between charity and public advocacy relatively late in life because of her early experiences in the convent:

We'd come out to teach, but, boy, we'd be back in that convent by 4:20 every afternoon so that we would say the prayers and all of that. And so, overwhelmingly, the message was not to be in the public arena, except to, like, let your light shine by good example, to be charitable to people and so forth. So, I didn't grow up in an environment at all to take on the public arena and get into the public sector and change systems.

Stretching in Both Directions

Sister Helen's testimony calls into question not only the adequacy of the "merely charitable" but also that of the exclusively systemic. In her view, doing public policy work without the essential personal anchor would be to err in the other direction. She was not alone in this conviction. Unprompted by me, half of the women leaders affirmed the strategy of keeping a foot in both modes — doing the ongoing dance between the particular and the universal.

For instance, when Jan Orr-Harter was pastor of an urban church with a large community outreach program, she was simultaneously a leader in the national freeze campaign to end the proliferation of nuclear weapons in the United States. Practicing the one-on-one systemic dance gave her energy:

> I was a local pastor engaged on both local and far-reaching issues, but always from a sort of local parish perspective. I never got so far into global things that I forgot the shut-ins' Communion. I was always able to stretch in both directions simultaneously, and those directions kind of stimulated and energized each other.

Lee Hancock, heading outreach ministries that focused on healing and AIDS/HIV issues, named the dance with both religious and political language:

> Howard Moody [former pastor of Judson Memorial Church in New York City] would talk about it as the movement between the pastoral and prophetic, to put it in that language. For me, it's the constant movement between policy (in the sense of thinking and clarifying what the issues are) and grassroots-based activism. By grassroots, I mean the place where you encounter people's lives. I'm really interested in the initiatives that rise up out of citizens' needs.

What's surprising about these accounts, especially to those accustomed to thinking of systemic work as the more effective means of social change, is the way the one-on-one work remains essential to the mix. It's not just something to be outgrown once the initial compelling encounters launch you to the next level. Let's look more closely at how one-on-one encounters contributed to the ongoing work.

The Power of Intimate Encounters

A Sustaining Nutrient

Recall that Gretchen Buchenholz, whom we met in chapter 1, pointed to her daily encounters with children as the source of the "motivational juice" critical to her sustenance. Touring one of her buildings after our interview, we passed dozens of children involved in various activities. Gretchen knew the name of every one. Other women in the study said they felt depleted when such personal encounters got crowded out by other duties as their organizations grew in size and complexity.

Ganga Stone started God's Love We Deliver after personally feeding one homebound person with AIDS. Over the course of nine years, the organization grew to the point where it fed several thousand persons a day. Ganga's days became filled with administration, fundraising, and interfacing with city government rather than delivering the food or pursuing the spiritual discipline described by Sister Prejean as "being with the suffering." Ganga said: "The thrill is gone, in the sense of 'I worship you with this food which I brought for you,' which was the wonderful experience of the initial years." She was a living demonstration of Sister Prejean's warning about being "once removed, twice removed, three times removed."

Other leaders, wistful about losing the touchstone of one-on-one encounters, spoke of reworking the balance of the dance in order to restore themselves. Laura Jervis remembered knowing everyone's name when she first founded West Side Federation for Senior Housing. Now with twelve buildings to manage and advocacy work around public policy, those intimate relationships are often sacrificed to the larger cause. Saying that it was harder to relate to abstract systems than to concrete human needs, she was playing with the idea that in the next phase of her career she might want to simply manage one building.

Alisa Del Tufo concurred. During the first twenty years of her professional career she has helped to found several organizations that address domestic violence through both direct services and social policy advocacy. Now she finds herself wanting to see change more vividly again, in the context of individual lives.

> I also feel like one of the things I am exhausted with right now is social change and policy reform. I think I've gone full circle. I started out doing direct service. What I want to do next is to work with individual people again. Not because of any other reason except that I somehow have gotten back to a place where I think that just helping individuals change when they are ready and want to change is a very big impact. And when you do policy change, you don't see much of that. And even when policies change, the people still have to get there. They still have to want the service, or be open to receiving it. Not to say that policy change isn't important, but just on my own personal trajectory, I am in a place where I feel like small groups or one-to-one is something I'm interested in doing.

These accounts suggest that working human-to-human and witnessing transformation in particular people's lives is a key source of satisfaction for these women and a critical safeguard against burnout. That these veteran social change professionals should want to re-emphasize it at the peak of their careers is a testament to its role as an essential nutrient and motivator. The trick is to stay balanced in the dance — to find and maintain the right mix of micro and macro activities.

Grounding the Abstract

Another aspect of the one-on-one encounter is its concreteness. For Rabbi Mychal Springer, this was an essential counterbalance to abstract policy work. In fact, when I interviewed her in her position as head of pastoral care in a large urban hospital, she insisted that working directly with patients and families was by far the more gratifying focus for her.

I've come to realize that I love things that are really concrete. It's kind of funny because the realm of the spirit is not concrete, but it becomes so when it's expressed in a particular story, particular individual. When things get too abstract and systemic, I get bored.

When asked to serve on a policy committee, Mychal initially declined, but then realized she was keenly interested in policies that she could connect with people she served.

It got me to thinking that there are very large issues that are connected to my work, issues of the ethics of healthcare — who gets cared for, what does it look like, what does it mean to be entitled to care, how do we treat one another? With all these mergers and partnerships, people being laid off, what does it mean to be responsible for one another?

She then reflected on how her work actually occurred in ever-expanding circles. Though she "began" with patients and their families, her desire to create a healing holding environment for them meant that she also addressed the ethos of the hospital itself. This entailed helping patients and staff become more comfortable discussing questions of meaning and the spiritual dimensions of life and death. Training student chaplains to do the same became a kind of "grassroots revolution," extending this quality of care to institutions all across the country who would someday hire them.

Justice as Right Relationship

"What does it mean to be responsible for one another?" Mychal's question captures the essence of these women leaders' ethical thinking. The word "respond" comes from the Latin *respondere* — to promise in return — as in "to make a solemn promise, pledge, betroth." Its ancient root is *spend,* which means to make an offering or perform a rite — to engage in a ritual act.[17] This suggests that one spends one's energies on behalf of others as part of a shared covenant. These women come to their sense of justice by seeing how current social policy plays out in people's lives. They understand justice as right relationship — as how we care for and respond to each other. Connie Baugh puts it this way in terms of her work in the criminal justice system:

> I've been able to get most of all my funders to understand justice as a right relationship. I've looked at other models of justice like retributive and this whole big thing on restorative justice. Restorative justice is fine, but I have a lot of problems with it, partly because they take the offender and they take the victim and they get them talking to each other and they want reconciliation. That's fine, but it's in the context of saying that the status quo is okay. What I'm working on is this model of transformative justice, which says, yes, you reconcile and you get the offender and the victim talking to one another, but you also analyze and change the structures and systems that perpetuate injustices.

For Mychal, Connie, and many others, individual stories are the pathway into broader thinking about ethics and social responsibility. When suffering and injustice have a particular name and face, they create a sense of accountability that cannot be ignored.

In my own evolving work with Face to Face/Faith to Faith, I am newly aware of this phenomenon. Experiencing the suffering of our teenage students, particularly those caught up in the Israeli-Palestinian conflict, has pressed me to engage with these issues on another level. At Auburn we have begun to convene a group of high-level business, political and religious leaders, academics, and activists to strategize about building a U.S. constituency for peace in that region, visible and viable enough to be seen and heard by our government here. A vigorous peace process with U.S. political and financial support must be vigilantly pursued, even in election years. I cannot know the children in our programs and tolerate less. Like Gretchen Buchenholz who had no experience as an activist, but had quarters to make a phone call, I have no knowledge or expertise in Middle East affairs, but I do know how to bring key people together to talk. This is what I can offer those children who deserve to live in peace. When I see them again I will be able to tell them what I am doing to do justice to our relationship. It is not really duty or principle or guilt which motivates me, but a feeling more like love. How can we in the United States better parent the future for these teens? What can we do to help them have safe homelands and a healthier world in which to body forth their dreams?

Moving Organically and Intuitively

Doing the one-on-one systemic dance moves these woman organically and intuitively to resist evil and to sponsor justice and healing all along a continuum that stretches from personal to global. Intimate personal work is an ongoing wellspring. Deprived of it, the women seem prone to compassion fatigue and burnout. Without the balance of the dance, their work feels to them disembodied, abstract, less genuine — in danger of becoming "a mere commentary" on the original, as Sister Prejean said. When clients' stories take root within the leaders, they become a lens for deciphering systemic dynamics, and a powerful motivation to act responsibly toward the relationship. Conversely, placing the personal within the larger context of the systemic confers meaning on personal struggles, casting them as modest yet precious triumphs in an ongoing global evolution toward justice for all.

From the Center Out:
A Woman's Mode of Ethical Action?

As I have begun to share this finding about the personal-systemic dance, I am discovering that it seems particularly resonant for women.

I think this is a clue to pursue. For instance, in a study of women leaders in corporate contexts, Sally Helgesen identifies a dynamic which has intriguing parallels. She calls it the "web of inclusion" because she finds these business women's mode of leadership to be based on web-like connections. She suggests that this image represents a new order emerging in our world.

> The notion of architecture is key here, for the science and art of architecture lie in skillfully relating individual parts to a greater whole, creating a form uniquely appropriate for a specific set of functions.... In architectural terms, the most obvious characteristics of the web are that it builds from the center out, and that this building is a never-ending process. The architect of the web works as a spider does, by ceaselessly spinning new tendrils of connection, while also continually strengthening those that already exist.[18]

As Helgesen points out, to be preoccupied with tendrils of connection is markedly different from traditional "top down" arrangements in male-dominated hierarchies. The web is built organically with a mix of rays and concentric pathways. Movement anywhere along a connecting tendril can be felt immediately everywhere else on the web. Think of the global information flow we now have over the connecting web of the Internet. We can witness change almost as soon as it occurs.

It strikes me that what the web and the dance have in common is a whole new physics of leverage — one which arises out of the discipline of attending to connections, to the nature and quality of relationship. When the personal and the systemic are felt to exist on a continuum, when every person is *simultaneously* a universe, change in one sphere changes the other. Models predicated on separation and domination do not measure change in this way. There, change is seen as stemming from positional power.

Returning to the question of making a difference, we can begin to detect not only a new physics but a new math afoot in the dance and the web. The bottom line is calculated differently. It is located not at the bottom of a hierarchy, but simultaneously at the center and periphery of the web. The bottom line is a measure of the number and strength of the tendrils of connection. Change happens and is measured through radiating webs of relationship rather than top-down power plays. It is measured in terms of how effectively the universe of person is put into right relationship with every other universe of person, regardless of where they sit on the web. In a concentric architecture, there is a shared center — a focus all parties hold in common (though perceive from different vantage points). Influence — leverage, change — occurs through back-and-forth responses in relation to that center, rather than who is on top of whom.

Why might this dynamic be so prominent a feature both in the corporate realm and in fields of social service and public policy? Is it an emerging mode of ethical action which is rooted particularly in the feminine principle? If we support this mode of seeing, responding, and acting, what sort of world will we make?

How much power does this mode have? Can the new physics of the web and the dance really bring about social transformation? To begin to answer these questions, we can look at how the women in my study learned to strategically leverage the energy of the dance.

Taking on the System

Diving Deeper

I had a dream recently when I was going through a particularly complex set of leadership challenges related to the Middle East peace conversations that I, with others, was trying to generate at Auburn. I dreamt I was swimming powerfully and forcefully through midnight blue water — an activity that I, poor swimmer that I am, would never normally choose. Whether I was human or part fish was unclear to me, so natural did the movement feel, and so competent did I feel doing it. Then a voice whispered to me: "Dive deeper!" I put my head under water, something I would normally never do, and found a fantastic world I had never seen. There were beautiful large fish — dolphins, whales, a host of unknown species — a world I might have missed had I not gone down.

This metaphor of going deeper is another way of looking at moving out from the center of the web and describes the natural movement that the women leaders made from intimate encounters with individuals to shaping institutions and influencing public policies and causes to which their concerns connected. Allowing themselves to be carried by the energy of the dance, they waded into the deeper waters suggested by the issues at hand, and, like me, took the plunge. It is not a once and for all event. It requires pacing, knowing one's limits, gaining strength, staying oriented, and coming up for air. But over time, given the repeated willingness to risk diving deeper, both stamina and savvy build.

Tactics from the Margins

Moving back and forth on the micro-macro continuum, the women leaders I spoke with gradually became complex, systemic thinkers, and have developed ways to use their organizations to apply leverage to some of the most intransigent social problems. What's more, they do so from their chosen positions on the margins of the mainstream. As we saw in chapter 2, their organizations function as holding environments which model and operate according to patterns of behavior distinctly different from those of society at large. Although these women leaders are CEOs, operating from the center of webs of their own design, they are almost by definition not operating from conventional centers of power.

Working at the margins calls for developing creative, unconventional strategies for change. The women I interviewed did this through a variety of tactics, often applied on a number of levels and fronts simultaneously. Alisa Del Tufo is one whose story touches on many of these.

Approaching Systems as People

In the early 1980s, after serving as the executive director of a battered women's shelter in New Jersey for a couple of years, she returned to New York and helped to found Sanctuary for Families, an organization initially designed to organize the religious community to provide shelter and legal assistance to abused women and their children, regardless of their income. Run out of a corner of a church building in Manhattan, it was initially primarily a Winnicott-style holding environment that literally offered a "safe" house for these women. Entering it, I felt enveloped by a compassionate chaos of clients and their children, social workers, bags of clothing, ringing phones, and volunteers. Like Helen Prejean, Alisa was clear that offering direct services was only part of the solution.

> I always thought that if you didn't engage the way the systems dealt with the problems, there would always be a thousand, million times more people who never got the services. So, it always seemed if you were interested in the issue from the perspective of social change as well as the perspective of direct care, you had to be involved on a more macro level.

Over the years, as she dove deeper into the stories her clients told her, Alisa realized that she wanted to refocus her efforts closer to the root of the problem. She wanted to take steps to prevent domestic violence from occurring in the first place. Sensing that this would entail challenging a certain amount of existing government policy, she felt uneasy about adding it to the work of Sanctuary for Families, since over a third of this organization's funding came from government grants. Also, the organization had grown large in its success and she missed the more direct connections with women she had once had. So she left Sanctuary in good hands and, in 1993, founded a new initiative — the Family Violence Project — which operates under the umbrella of a non-profit collaborative called the Urban Justice Center. This project functions more as a Heifetz-style holding environment in that, through education and advocacy, it seeks to carry whole systems and groups toward new behaviors.

But even as she made this shift in emphasis, Alisa did so in a way that humanized the system. Her philosophy is to approach systems as if they are persons, offering them sensitivity, patience, and respect.

> I think individual people can change, and I also guess I believe systems can change. I think I approach the systems with the same kind of commitment to them as I would to an individual — the same kind of perseverance, the same kind of respect for their integrity.

Here we see striking evidence of a belief that the personal and the systemtic are of the same stuff, that they exist on a continuum and respond to the same laws of physics. Also expressed here is one of the key attributes of these women leaders: a belief in the possibility of transformation for both individuals and systems. Holding this conviction is a key ingredient in actually effecting change.

Persistent Patience with Resistance

Perseverence is needed because systems and people alike often resist deep change. Decades of patience are sometimes required. Alisa offered this example:

We've shown that between 60 and 70 percent of all the mothers of kids in the child welfare system are battered. That's a lot. And yet, because of all sorts of complex mental and emotional and political reasons, the child welfare system has not yet really said, "Okay, you're right, we need to really change this." Because they know that if they really accept it, they'd have to change the way they do almost everything, and who wants to do that? I mean, we're not saying, "Oh, well, if you just do this a little differently over here, everything will be fine." It's so deep and it's so many people and it has so many different layers of importance that you have to change a lot of the way you do your work. And that's just what I'd like them to do. So when I started doing this I realized I was probably going to be working on this issue for at least a decade — or more.

How does she convince resistant systems that proposed changes will work? Primarily through pilot projects — miniature versions of systems working according to the new patterns of behavior. "Pilot projects can be evaluated and can demonstrate real impact on the way these cases are adjudicated." But she feels other leverage must simultaneously be brought to bear:

> I think you have to go about that kind of change at a million different levels. So another level is harassing the commissioner and the mayor, and another is trying to find allies high enough up within the child welfare system that you can begin to change their points of view, or shaming [public officials] by getting publicity on cases that show that ignoring these connections harms children — because that's who they care about.

Her core strategy when trying to encourage systems or people to face deep challenges is to begin by engaging them where they are, a concept she borrows from Paulo Freire.

You try to deal with them in a way that respects their place in the world, their sense of what's right. Because most people come to you with their own set of beliefs that they're doing the right thing.... So I try to engage people with the central issue in a way that doesn't diminish them, in a way that offers this experience as a way to open up and to transform.

Being present to the complexity and darkness of issues like domestic violence can be taxing. Yet it is part of the make-up of the social alchemist to know the potential value of it, and to summon the energy to keep moving through the dark.

It's very hard for them. You have to be prepared to be confronted with very defensive and negative attitudes toward women. I can't help but get a little bit rattled by that. It costs a lot to do all of this stuff, but you just keep thinking, how do you worm your way in there to get them to think that it might be a good idea to do something differently? You're not really sure what takes and for whom. But it's like gardening, you plant the seed. You hope that sometimes they take hold.

Her ultimate goal is "capacity-building": developing within large public service agencies a better understanding of the causes and effects of domestic violence so that they will be able to identify abused women and more effectively help them, even when this is not the presenting problem. She conducts ongoing research into the dynamics of domestic abuse with the victims themselves. "If you're going to develop policy that's really going to help people, you have to know what's happening to them on the street, not what some demographic study shows. That's why you have to do oral history or direct service as well as policy." Recent studies, for instance, helped identify the most likely moments when a woman might consider leaving an abusive situation — when she becomes aware that her children are being affected and when she begins to fear that she is about to become violent herself. Now, diving yet another layer deeper, she is wondering if she can understand and change the batterers themselves.

> For years, all I've thought about is how to stop them, period. But as a believer in transformation, now I'm beginning to think, well, how would you transform these guys who don't even see it as a problem?

Alisa has sustained a level of passion for the issue of domestic violence over decades, becoming an expert in the field. She has created a holding environment that shines an intense light on this particular public issue through multiple, mutually reinforcing elements that are themselves interconnected: gaining alliances with influential people, harassing public officials, launching pilot projects to demonstrate success, research and capacity-building to make advocates out of related public agencies. She has become agile at thinking deeply and constantly on many levels at once, creating feedback loops which shore up deficiencies at one level with insight from another. Her comprehensive approach, offering support and challenge to systems and individuals alike, is a strategically organized system unto itself, graciously sensitive to the resistance to change, but fiercely patient to achieve it.

Relying on Ripples

Diving deeper, like throwing the proverbial pebble into a pond, does indeed set in motion a series of ripples which extend in ever-widening circles. It is a testament to the women leaders' conviction about the continuum between personal and systemic that they so clearly rely on the ripple effect to help create widespread social transformation. They trust the power of the intimate encounter to create life-altering change, human to human, in ever-expanding numbers, until our whole sense of how to be together — "what it means to be responsible for one another" — is so transformed that we naturally begin to capture it in the very systems we construct to institutionalize our values.

What a contrast this is to the diminished sense of individual agency with which many of us labor, doubting that our actions and choices can ever make a dent in "the way things are." These women leaders are aware of how easily paralyzed we all are by the seeming immensity of the task. Sensitive to the need to demonstrate results, they often employ a modest, human-scale approach because it's doable, and therefore encouraging. Jan Orr-Harter, Presbyterian minister and peace activist, told me about approaching a grand vision through a series of feasible steps.

> You have to be the good news. You have to be willing to work on a difficult issue with love in your heart and not make people feel judged or depressed or immobilized.... Your skill is making people feel that they can do something about it.... I felt that you couldn't organize for world peace, per se, couldn't use that grand language. There had to be middle axioms and middle-ground progress. So rather than organizing for world peace, I was organizing to cut the military budget back to its pre-1970s size and not build the next generation of nuclear weapons. These were much more gradualist, politically feasible steps. They were still big steps, but they could be accomplished by human beings.

Transforming Tea into Dolls: The Power of Grassroots Momentum

As the Swiss railway system so convincingly demonstrates, some of the world's highest and most rugged terrain can be scaled at a feasible, gradual rate, cog by sturdy cog. These women alchemists perform similar feats in people's hearts, relying on the sheer contagious power of a good idea. This is how Linda Tarry-Chard transmuted a cup of tea into fifteen thousand dolls and an economic development model for impoverished women worldwide. For those of you still concerned about "scope" and the "bottom line," be advised that the pebble at the center of this story is one woman, assisted by one part-time employee. (The question of how life conspired to groom Linda as this most efficacious pebble is one that I shall return to in chapter 8.)

The immediate circumstance that primed Linda for this work was a seventeen-day tour of South Africa she took with an Episcopal church group in January 1995. They met with Bishop Desmond Tutu and witnessed firsthand the legacy of apartheid. Within weeks of her return to New York, Linda received a phone call from Diane Steinman of the American Jewish Committee, asking her to meet with Helen Lieberman, a white Jewish South African who had been doing social service work in the black townships under the old regime, even though doing so was illegal. Given the new political circumstances, Helen was trying to develop support for the work here in the United States. Though Linda felt too busy at the time, she agreed to meet with Helen as a favor to Diane. What started as a half-hour cup of tea became three hours in a restaurant and a pledge to help Helen collect and distribute fifteen thousand black dolls for children in the townships — children who had never before held a likeness of themselves in their arms because none was available in their homeland.

It took Linda less than a year to fulfill this pledge, but by then the work had a momentum that morphed it into something of a different order — a self-reliance initiative that would begin to address the conditions Linda had witnessed on her trip to South Africa:

The Black Doll Project just evolved into Project People Foundation — a community development, social justice, economic justice program, which ended up creating work with a doll factory, and women creating black dolls in the townships of South Africa for retail sale there, as well as export to this country. And in this country we market them under what I love to think of as "doll giveaway" — a charitable program called Sponsor a Smile. For every $20 donated, we buy a doll and give it to a child in need. And this doll giveaway is in countries all over the world. We give to Ethiopian children in Israel, South African children in the townships, and to needy African-American children here. And that market is expanding.

The program was so successful in South Africa that Linda decided to replicate it in impoverished areas of the United States, both rural and urban, as Crafting Social Change.

"Just evolved" is the key phrase here. It sounds like it's happening by itself with no one in charge. But Linda made it clear that even grassroots growth needs to be watched and channeled. "It has been a project that has grown, but grown with direction. Not just grown like a weed, but very much nurtured and cultivated, thinking through who we would work with, how we would get from one point to another. But there is always a spirit that just seems to envelop this project and move it from one point to another."

In a hierarchical structure, power is positional, based on role. Who you are and who you know matters. The people with "clout" are the ones who "make things happen." In the concentric world of webs, or along the personal-systemic continuum, it doesn't matter who you are — not in the sense of your power quotient. But it does matter who you know — all the people you talk to, human to human, about this compelling idea you've just heard. And then it matters how your heart responds, and how you determine to apply the sensibilities and skills you happen to have to the job at hand. That's what makes the grassroots grow.

Linda was speaking about Project People at Syracuse University. An affluent white woman from Arkansas was on campus visiting her son and heard her. She was so moved that when she returned home she immediately went to purchase a few black dolls to donate. When she arrived at the cash register, the person at the counter was baffled by her choice and asked if she really wanted them. In her entire life as a consumer, no one had ever asked her such a question.

That put her in a place she had never been before. She went back to her church and shared this with the women's group, who, as a response, all wanted to go out and buy black dolls. And what they found out was that there weren't that many available. That made them probe a little deeper. There were white dolls everywhere. Why were there so few black dolls? And it made them look at themselves and how they had lived, and start to ask questions. Do our children, as white children, play with black dolls? And they began to really look at that.

This woman then became Project People's volunteer coordinator for Arkansas.

Then there is the case of the young man who arrived at Linda's tiny office to install a computerized payroll system:

He's a kid twenty-five years old. He wants to know why all these black dolls are sitting around. I tell him the story. He immediately takes out a piece of paper and says, "Is it all right if I give your name and number to my mother? I know she'd love this." Well, he went home and told her just second-hand what I had told him. She calls me and says, "My son never gets this excited about anything. He went on and on and on. I'd love to meet you. What are you doing?" Turns out she's a major force in the garment industry. Her office is walking distance from my home. She's meeting me in my home next week, and she has wonderful ideas for design of clothing for the dolls.

Back at the initial cup of tea, who could have known?

Tapping into Mainstream Power

While these women have had notable success with grassroots movement, they are also pragmatic enough to use whatever works, even if this entails some dangerous alliances. Sometimes linking up with the people with clout seems the best means to achieve the desired effect. Laura Jervis, for instance, over the course of twenty years, had converted twelve city buildings into viable housing for several thousand poor and homeless people. But at a particularly critical juncture involving policy change, she recognized the limits of her authority. She and her cabal of women colleagues and friends who regularly strategized about issues of leverage realized that Cardinal O'Connor, a highly respected leader, might be the best person to call together a multifaith constituency to focus on issues of homelessness and other social ills. As she explained it:

> We felt that they weren't going to do it themselves, so we'd have to set it up so that they would do it, because it's so important to have a moral voice out there. [Other prominent male religious leaders in New York City] don't have the energy or focus for it. We're single issue on homelessness.... The gap is widening between rich and poor. It is desperate, and we are shameless, and we are really trying to manipulate and focus the Cardinal on this particular issue.

It was a risky move, for there were a number of issues on which Laura and the Cardinal had divergent views — a woman's right to choose, city legislation about recognizing gay and lesbian relationships as legitimate partnerships, among others. As it turned out, the Cardinal did deliver a homily on the right to decent housing which had a major impact on the mayor's thinking.

Jan Orr-Harter also has a reputation as an astute pragmatist who has worked to make strategic alliances with men in power on the issue of nuclear disarmament — former Senator Alfonse D'Amato among them. When several attempts to meet with him were deflected, Jan gathered the support of a thousand people to lobby outside his office in Washington until he met with her. Jan's underlying conviction about working with political people is that it is important to emphasize their power to make a difference, to activate their deeper sense of calling and agency as a politician while simultaneously offering the more typical motivators of "numbers of people, the groups, the endorsements." An ordained minister and strong leader in her own right, Jan still felt she could not accomplish her aims without fully engaging with politicians and the political process.

> It's not a matter of the church saving the world. . . . The world has got to change and rearrange itself. In my view the church is not the steeple, the church is the ground, and so that church has to get underneath the politicians and push them to do the right thing. . . . You have to assume that the God that is in anybody can be the one to do it, and it's probably not the God in you that's going to do it. The church is just the servant under the ground, and the politicians have to get out in front of the people and claim the credit. That's how the world changes.

The willingness to make alliances with powerful men is an interesting strategy on a number of levels. It is a time-honored tactic that has historical and biblical precedents because women throughout history have been and continue to be marginalized. The fact that this reality still exists reinforces the need to work for women's full participation in positions of leadership, public and otherwise. I was surprised to find religious leaders willing to acknowledge these strategies as a way to leverage power on particular issues. Yet Jan's theological rationale is fascinating because it depicts a creative partnership between religious and political forces. On the one hand it acknowledges the limitations of religious leaders given our current cultural context. At the same time it identifies a public and political role for them as people who can initiate alliances and influence those who are in positions of power. Jan's words have come back to me often as I realize that unconsciously we are using this exact tactic in our Middle East peace work, forming alliances around this particular issue with religious, business, academic, and political leaders. Our steering committee — composed of both men and women — has adopted as a strategy seeking out political leaders and convincing them of the importance of this work.

Self-Taught Strategists

We live in a world, particularly here in the United States, where size matters. The efficacy of an undertaking is often measured by the probability of large-scale impact, the consequence being that many of us are overwhelmed before we begin. These women leaders seemed to employ a different kind of calibration and sense of proportion, realizing that the important thing is to start somewhere, trusting that through hard work and collaboration the impact will eventually grow.

The discovery of the one-on-one systemic dance and its relationship to Helgesen's web of inclusion — both metaphors for the interplay between the micro and macro — continues to fascinate me. I realize that unconsciously I have been employing it in my own work for some time. More broadly, I wonder if it may be a leadership discipline or best practice that is key to nourishment and the avoidance of burnout.

Before studying these women I had little appreciation for the complexity of their systemic work. Exercising responsibility over the long haul, in the sense of fulfilling a sacred covenant with other human beings, requires proficiency and adaptability. I was unprepared for their expertise as practical strategists, attacking social problems from many angles at once: direct services, pilot projects, grassroots coalitions, alliances with power, advocacy, lobbying, research, and education. All the more remarkable is the fact that none of these leaders had been formally educated to her task. Most learned to be strategists for change through intuition and on-the-job experimentation.

What is clear from examining these patterns of work is that these leaders are doers and activists. Unaccustomed as they are to talking about their lives and work, they found the interviews a rare opportunity to "dive below the surface," to take stock and reflect on their leadership practices. As we shall see in the next chapter, they surprised me again in how they understood, analyzed, and described their roles as leaders.

Chapter 4

LEADING FROM BEHIND, WITHIN, AND BENEATH

There are whole projects these days — non-profit machines deploying public relations staffs, fundraisers, and spenders — to help women leaders gain greater prominence and visibility. Marie Wilson, for instance, through the work of the Ms. Foundation, has dedicated several decades of her life to nurturing women's leadership in contexts ranging from the grassroots to the top echelons. Now as President of the White House Project, her goal is more targeted still — through research, education, and advocacy to elect women leaders to public office, building a critical mass toward that magic day when we actually have a woman head of state. While India, England, Pakistan, and Israel, to name a few, have already achieved this goal, it still eludes us here in the United States despite the great strides of the feminist movement. Some religious institutions like Auburn Seminary have parallel endeavors. Our Glass Ceiling Project is one such attempt to grow a pool of gifted women ministers, particularly good at preaching, to become senior ministers of large and prominent churches — a goal that few have attained thus far.

While the goals of such projects are often framed in terms of putting a woman in a traditional position of power, I see this as a shorthand for a broader societal hunger — the desire for fundamentally different leadership *behavior.* This, I believe, is a shift which men and women alike find promising, intriguing, sometimes difficult to trust, yet compelling. But we need to take care lest our shorthand obscure the vision.

That is, embedded in such shorthand is a critical assumption: that there is a difference between putting a woman in the White House who behaves like a man, and putting one there who behaves like a woman. To state it this way may be inflammatory and polarizing, but it does highlight the magnitude of the transformation before us if we truly want to be led by people who embody values traditionally identified with the feminine principle.

If we are to feed this hunger, we need to begin to make room in our minds for new images of leadership, broadening our sense of what kinds of behaviors count as leadership. And we need to realize the degree to which traditional notions of power continue to act upon us as a kind of undertow, sometimes undermining our instinct to experiment with alternative behaviors. I know this because the interviews I had with women leaders surprised me by becoming a time for all of us to bump up against our ingrained assumptions about leadership, even as we strove to name and enact new modes.

That's Not the Kind of Leader I Am

I had chosen these twenty women because to my eye they were effective leaders doing notable public work. They continue to speak publicly as expert witnesses in legislative arenas, as preachers, or as advocates for social change. Many have won awards for their leadership, written books, founded and led organizations and movements. While I was particularly curious about whether and how they envisioned themselves as religious leaders, I prefaced that discussion with two more general questions: *What does the word leader mean to you?* and *Do you consider yourself a leader?*

I had assumed that all of them would readily claim the designation of leader in a secular sense, but that some might not think of their approach as religious in the narrower sense. But their answers surprised me. When I asked, *Do you consider yourself a leader?* there was a notable pause. Very few latched onto the title easily but instead began offering qualifiers and expanded definitions. It seems that the term "leader," perhaps like the term "feminist," has become problematic, especially for women. Just as there is now something that presses people to say that they are not *that* kind of feminist but *this* kind, the women I spoke with wanted to distance themselves from certain connotations of leadership — like being out front, alone, and in command — and define the word on their own terms. Here is how that sounded.

> I guess there are different types of leaders. There are people who have really strong public personas and are, like famous leaders, people with real extroverted personalities who can speak to large groups of people and motivate them to do something. That's incredible, and that's not the kind of leader I am, by far. Maybe that's an alpha leader or something, but that's not me. I'm not saying that I don't have a strong ego and I don't have some kind of charisma that people feel, but it's not that kind. It's much more a roll-up-my-sleeves and work *with* people kind. Not so much that big personality person.

Others also stressed the element of collaboration, in various ways locating themselves within the group they were leading. Gretchen, whom we met in chapter 1, insisted: "I don't see leadership as an alone thing. I only see myself as a leader when I join with other people in the community who see the issue first or get up and do it first." Echoing this, another said:

> Leader? I don't know, that's a tough word. I don't consider myself a leader. I consider myself a doer, and if what I happen to be doing is the right thing and people agree with that, then we can go in the same direction.

Lee Hancock, drawing upon her years of work organizing community health programs, challenged the traditional command and control image and offered an alternative from the arts:

I think there is a lot in our corporate mentality about leadership being my way and top down. I'm not like that at all. I think leadership is not about being a control freak whatsoever. In fact, I think that's killing. I think a good metaphor for leadership is the conductor of a symphony, who understands the piece of music, knows how he or she wants to interpret it, and then is able to call forth the best from each member of the orchestra and help them weave together their part with the others.[19]

Another of the women said simply: "I think a leader is a person who creates community."

These responses reflect the desire to see one's efforts in the company of others, a preference for a sense of collaboration, and less emphasis on being a "big personality" out front. I noticed that this spatial shift was key to many of the women leaders. They were willing to claim themselves as leaders only as they changed the architecture of the image.

Behind, Within, and Beneath

Mindy Fullilove, a prominent and innovative theorist in the field of urban community health, initially shied away from the term leader because she felt that organizing people was not her strong suit. Her gifts, she felt, had to do with thinking. But then she offered me this image of what it meant to be a leader in thought — the one who has maverick ideas — a role with which she strongly identified:

Do you remember the scene in the first Indiana Jones movie? He's in the cave, and the guy with the light is behind him; the light is shining over his shoulder. I feel like the guy with the light.

With excitement, she was recognizing as we spoke that this image captures the way her work feels to her. Though she is not literally the one in front, and is often working in tandem with the nominative leader, she is in fact the one showing the way—*leading from behind*. Research and writing, when they name a new and promising path, are indeed forms of leadership.

Barbara Dobkin, philanthropist and founder of Ma'yan, a project to reconceive Judaism from a feminist perspective, readily thinks of herself as a leader. Yet she too offered an image that emphasizes the value of occasionally leading from behind. "A leader to me," she said, "is a person who knows how to share leadership." She told me of a woman rabbi who she felt did this well: "This was a woman who could come up front and take responsibility, but who knew when to step back and lead from the back. I mean, she was still leading, but people didn't know she was doing it. It was sort of leading without ego." Barbara finds this from-the-back mode particularly valuable for cultivating the leadership of younger women in the organizations with which she is associated. What Barbara is alluding to is one of the arts of leadership, fluidly shifting one's locus of leadership in a way that makes room for the capabilities of others in the group.

Jan Orr-Harter, the urban minister whom we met in chapter 3, uses an image of leadership which includes theological reflection and literally stands the traditional notion of leadership on its head:

I think of the leader at the bottom of the organizational chart, the one whose name is at the bottom of the letterhead. And in a way you have to be willing to let some stuff be built on your shoulders. You're standing on somebody else's shoulders, so you've got to let others stand on yours when you're the leader. I always feel like one leads from underneath the institution, providing structure and support. And I'm a very up-front, out-front person. I do a lot of public work, but I perceive it as coming from underneath. It's just how I perceive God as being down below, not above. I really do have a sense of God pushing and pulling me through. In public work, like in the peace movement, you have to do all sorts of risky things. But you just hold onto God's hand, and you do it. My theology has always been of God underneath, not above.

This image depicts the leader as a builder whose very being is also part of the architecture, as is God's energy. God is not the grand puppeteer looking down from on high, but is instead a steadying, generative, enabling force akin to what theologian Paul Tillich called the "ground of being."

How Much Ego Is Enough?

These accounts reveal a marked preference for leading in collaboration with others and from locations other than those to which we are accustomed. Only one woman characterized her style as more masculine, saying that she thought like a man and had always identified with her father. I wondered if for the others there was some sort of politically correct ethos at work. As our discussion unfolded, were these women concerned to portray themselves as feminist leaders, distinct from their male counterparts? Were we all getting caught by the desire to give evidence of the egalitarian and progressive values we say we hold? To what degree do we actually succeed at living them?

A related question arises: does reluctance to being out front and alone constitute a strength or a finessed weakness? That is, are these women actively choosing to lead from behind, within, and beneath because of a conviction that this is more effective, or do they do it out of fear of what leading from the front may entail? A way to respond to such questions is to explore what role ego plays in leadership and how it functions in what we might call the beta form of leadership that these women say they prefer. To lead effectively, how much ego does one need?

The word "ego" actually surfaced in a number of interviews, often as something negative. Recall how Barbara Dobkin characterized the rabbi's willingness to shift between the front and back of the group as "leading without ego." Ganga Stone, founder of God's Love We Deliver, a program to provide food to housebound people suffering from HIV/AIDS, carried this even further.

> The job I had before this one was selling coffee and pastry on the street. It's very hard to have grandiose notions of yourself after you've been doing that. So by the time I was actually in a leadership position, there wasn't any "I am the leader" left in me, which is of course what God would have you do; otherwise you're not qualified, at least not to do a ministry like this. (That's why when you hear a preacher whose every other word is a first person pronoun, you know right away that this is somebody who should not be in the pulpit at this time.)

Preachers beware! Ganga went on to tell me a dream she had had which helped her to know that she was ready to exercise this "egoless" leadership. It depicted her as "silently serving" with no "I am" emphasis and no "lust for glory and recognition." This, to her, was the ideal — a preference which may stem from her extensive study and practice of Eastern religions. Embedded here is the assumption that alpha-type leaders have big egos. The question is whether such egos are appropriately sized for the role or inflated in a way that jeopardizes the work.

Some of the other women associated ego with insisting that things be done "my way," or more generally, with a desire to remain in control. One even acknowledged with a conspiratorial laugh that inside she is actually a "dictator of the first order." Reflecting on how her leadership had evolved in the course of twenty years, Laura Jervis noted that at first it had been hard for her to cede control, but as her organization grew larger and more complex, she had learned to delegate authority. Motivating her, in part, was her growing awareness of the risks of one person being the sole direction setter: "I read someplace a very scary thing that I didn't like at all — that an organization only rises as high as its leader's vision." Yet even though she considers the lone leader "too individualistic a notion" to embrace, she still does not just give over to group process:

> I mean, obviously, there is a tension within me about that because I do feel like I'm in charge, but I don't want to think of [my organization] as being solely dependent on me. I work very hard to ensure that's not the case and to promote a real sharing of responsibility.

Here she has named one of the paradoxes of effective leadership: learning the right mix of holding on and letting go. Sharing authority and leading from the back seem to involve less ego, yet have the effect of strengthening the group, freeing others to become more deeply engaged, more able to offer their insights and skills to the challenge at hand.

Notably absent from these women's definitions of leadership was a desire for power as a form of personal clout. Lee Hancock told me that it is not power that motivates her, but the thrill of the creative process:

> Some secular people cannot understand my vision of leadership at all, and cannot understand how I use power. They always project upon me that I am going to be controlling, or that it's about gaining more and more personal political power. I'm really not motivated that way. There's another kind of person who wants to exercise power and leadership through back door dealing, private conversations. I will not do that. I'm a person of process and openness. It's just a very different leadership style, and part of it really does come out of my religious conviction, which is that people matter and I want to hear their voices.
>
> I'm also motivated by the process of actualizing a vision. That's an act of creativity for me which turns me on and feels very

exciting. I truly can say that's much more gratifying for me than becoming a godfather.

Something Bigger in the Room

In this mode of leadership, then, the desire to hear other people's voices and share responsibility tempers the urge to have one's own way. This image, however, contrasts sharply with how we usually think of entrepreneurs — as single-minded risk-takers fueled by 24/7 energy. In fact, it flies in the face of what I have observed over the course of many years about how at least some of these women lead. I had chosen them because they had demonstrated initiative and courage. Without these strengths, they could not have created and shaped the organizations they had. Yet now they were telling me that partners were essential to the process. Helen Hunt, founder and president of The Sister Fund, was one of several who made me realize that it was not single-mindedness and force of personality they relied upon, but collective wisdom. The creator of several women's funds for grassroots projects to empower women and girls, Helen said she took a cue from the Ms. Foundation and began to design decision-making bodies which were diverse in composition.

> [The Ms. Foundation] was the first, and they developed a board that was cross-racial, cross-cultural, cross-socioeconomic. Instead of elite people making the decisions about the allocation of funds, they had women from the community at all levels decid-ing about the allocation of funds. . . . I modeled the Sister Fund after the public funds in terms of commitment to a cross-racial, cross-cultural board. So there are ten of us on the board, and I have one vote and get voted down a lot. But the joy of work-ing collaboratively exceeds the times that I don't get to stay in control . . . because I don't trust a single perspective like I do a collective perspective. So, when things aren't going my way, I just

go, "Well, there's a collective wisdom here, and there's something bigger than me in the room right now."

That "something bigger in the room" — the reminder it is that one's own perspective is only one part of a much larger picture — seems to be the key to keeping one's ego the right size. I think it is a misnomer to call this egoless leadership. It is not that one needs to have no ego to participate in such a process; it is that one needs an ego that is conscious of its limits and vulnerabilities. As Carl Jung and other theorists have noted, this sense of self usually does not take root until midlife or beyond — and even then not in everyone. Its essential characteristic is a paradoxical mix of both deference and hubris, and includes a deep respect for how much one does not know and cannot control. As Jung has written, it involves a kind of surrender of ego to something larger — a defeat in one sense — and yet makes possible a significant gain — the possibility of finding one's unique place in the mystery of things.

> The decisive question for man is: Is he related to something infinite or not? That is the telling question of his life. The feeling for the infinite, however, can be attained only if we are bounded to the utmost. Only consciousness of our narrow confinement in the self forms the link to the limitlessness of the unconscious. In such awareness we experience ourselves concurrently as limited and eternal, as both the one and the other. In knowing ourselves to be unique — that is, ultimately limited — we possess also the capacity for becoming conscious of the infinite. But only then![20]

Here is where the hubris comes in. It is the willingness to serve as a conduit for creative energies, to play one's small but essential role in manifesting visions or unraveling complexities which exceed any one person's grasp. It is a sense of self which remains *in relation to* the infinite — in ongoing dialogue with mystery — but avoids the dual dangers of being conflated with it (inflation) or obliterated by it (deflation). It dares to believe it has a meaningful role to play even as the minute speck in the cosmos it knows it is.

This is one way of answering the question, "How much ego is enough?" I think it names something of the spirit with which these women leaders approach collaborative leadership and why they are learning to trust collective wisdom even more than their own. At its best, collaborative leadership moves toward a full embodiment of this elusive sense of self which truly trusts the essential contributions of diverse unique perspectives. Rather than a big ego, it calls for a mature and balanced one, cognizant of its potential role in a larger process and tempered by a lived knowledge of its own vulnerabilities.

This helps explain the apparent dichotomy between entrepreneurial activity and the ability to orchestrate and depend upon the gifts of others to achieve goals. Given this, it is more accurate to say that these women are being entrepreneurs in an even broader sense than I first realized. With their ego balancing act and behind-within-beneath leverage, they are not only building new organizations, they are also enacting a new leadership *process* — disrupting our assumptions and helping us to recast the image of leadership itself.

Alpha Leader Undertow

But there are seductions and pitfalls along the way. I am suggesting that what these women leaders are trying to name is a "best practice" mode with which they have had success but which they are not always able to achieve. Sometimes this came up explicitly in the interviews; in other cases it seemed implied. I am familiar with this mixed mode phenomenon from watching my own and others' leadership of late, and am aware of several contributing factors.

First, having the kind of balanced ego stance I am describing requires ongoing attention and adjustment. There are continuing pressures to tip toward inflation or deflation. A host of shadowy or less mature impulses beckon or overtake us. For example, even though ideologically I support the notion of collaborative leadership, particularly among my "sisters," my actions often fall far short of the ideal. I sometimes use the leverage of a top-down hierarchy or get drawn into compare/compete dynamics, particularly with other women, assessing my progress in the success game by seeing how I measure up. Playing this game means doing what it takes to look the part — tweaking one's clothing and physical appearance, acquiring the right mix of professional accomplishments, and demonstrating that one is well-connected and personally content. The list of accoutrements goes on and on, varying with context. Yet instead of connecting with others in a way that makes everyone feel valued, playing this competitive game becomes alienating, isolating, and finally defeating.

Along with these shadowy ego traps, there is the considerable undertow of our traditional image of leadership. We fall into alpha-leader patterns, or even deliberately choose them, because they represent culturally legitimized modes of behavior. For centuries, we have equated them with leadership. Particularly for many women, there is the enervating pressure to favor an intellectual mode over the emotional. An especially prevalent pressure for all who lead is to be an expert in the matter at hand. Especially in crisis, or when confronted with complex challenges, we appropriately seek insight from authorities in the field. How can they offer what they do know while preserving for all of us the reality of what they do not? Are they secure enough to reveal to us the partialness of their expertise, and are we prepared to let them — prepared that is, to be left with the problem still in our midst?

Though a raft of leadership books now point toward various non-alpha modes as more appropriate to our shifting global context,[21] particularly for what Ronald Heifetz has called adaptive challenges — that is, the ones for which there *are* no ready answers, even from experts — none of us are very practiced in actually behaving them. To a greater degree than we realize, the old myths still hold sway in our psyches even as they begin to crumble. It takes considerable strength to resist their undertow and live into a new myth — in effect to help coagulate it in our imaginations by experimenting with alternative behaviors which we intuit as promising. These women leaders offer us examples of that form of strength, even if only in glimpses. As the culture experiences it and begins to trust its efficacy, many more of us will be able to more confidently name and choose it as leadership.

Sometimes the necessary strength is closer than we think — a matter of a shift in perspective. If we look more closely at expertise, we find that its root is *per*, which means to try, risk, or press forward, and that it carries connotations of danger.[22] It also means to learn by trying, as in experiment. In our modern crises, we may find strength by re-rooting ourselves in this ancient understanding of expertise as being more process than product. An expert is not someone who has all the answers, but is someone who is willing to press forward in a mode of ·informed experimentation, learning as she goes.

Learning Interdependence

As we move toward such reframed images of leadership, we need to be patient with our loss of balance, our reversion to familiar patterns. We are engaged with a considerable learning curve. Educational psychologists would say that what we are doing is negotiating a critical shift in consciousness. We are learning the radically interconnected and interdependent nature of our world. We are learning that we cannot merely give this concept lip-service. We actually need to trust and practice it as if our lives depend on it. Because they do.

As educator and theorist Sharon Parks describes it, interdependence significantly recasts the dynamics of power and authority:

> This transformation constitutes another qualitative shift in the balance of vulnerability, trust, and faith. Now more at home with both the limitations and the strengths of the self, one can be at

home with the truth embedded in the strengths and limitations of others. A person's center of primary trust now resides neither in the assumed authority of another, nor in the courageously claimed authority of the inner self. Rather, trust is now centered in the meeting of self and other, in the recognition of the strength and finitude of each, and in the promise of the truth that emerges in relation. This trust takes the form of a profound, self-aware conviction of interdependence.

...Dwelling in this conviction of interdependence makes it possible to depend upon others without fear of losing the power of the self.... The person now most trusts the truth that emerges in the dialectic, or, better, in the communion between self and other, self and world, self and "God."[23]

Herein is the paradox that when we know and claim our own vulnerabilities, we actually enjoy a stronger, more resilient, more open sense of being. We can collaborate with others non-defensively, affirming differing contributions rather than setting them in competition.

Ginny Thornburgh for instance, gave me a wonderful window on this as she described the early days of creating a national program to help congregations welcome people with disabilities. She came to this work with plenty of experience, including a lifetime as a mother to her brain-injured son, many years of community work on disability issues, and a stint at Harvard as coordinator of programs for persons with disabilities. Yet she was well aware that doing this work within faith communities meant entering new territory.

I didn't know anything — how to begin, what to do — I just knew I wanted to do it. So we pulled together a group of people we knew who were religious people interested in disability. Then as I talked to people on the phone I realized there was lots of stuff I didn't know. I remember day four getting a call from a mom whose son had not been admitted to the bar mitzvah classes and she wanted to know if the rabbi had a right to exclude her son. Well, here is Miss Presbyterian sitting at her desk saying, "Well, I'm in a time bind right now," which of course I wasn't, "but it's an important question and let me get back to you, please." Well, I had begun to collect people from a variety of faiths to ask advice from. So I called my friend who's a special ed teacher and wife of a rabbi, and she gave me four references to give to that mom. It just shows how much I didn't know and how people have come forward to support me.

And then she ended the story in a way that reveals the full trust in interdependence that the ensuing years have given her: "Now I would just say to the mom, 'Gee, I don't know, but I know somebody who does.'"

In fact, this ability to honor the strengths of both self and others meshes well with leading from the back. I think of my desire to make a difference in the Middle East, despite the gaps in my knowledge and experience. I want to create a space for conversation among high-level leaders about the Israeli-Palestinian conflict. Under Auburn's auspices, we have periodically gathered religious and business leaders, academics and politicians to explore how to develop a visible, viable U.S. constituency focused on a peaceful solution to the conflict. Before the initial meeting, I thought about how I wanted to "be" in that setting. The alpha-leader undertow began to take effect. I found myself thinking that I wanted to be visible — to make sure that I sounded smart, that others knew without a shadow of a doubt that I had been, at least in part, responsible for getting that group together. I was leading with too much ego. But with the help of a colleague, I shifted toward a beta-leadership mode which actually felt more authentic. I did this by allying myself with the urges coming from my deeper core: to create a welcoming, nurturing environment, to be a good "mother" to the process, to deploy heart as well as mind. It came to me that I would try to "be peace" in the room in order that others might find a peaceful center within themselves, even as we engaged passionate and divergent ideas.

It worked — or that was the feedback. A Palestinian Christian businessman who had participated in hundreds of such meetings commented on the absence of conflict and tension, and therefore the presence of hope. In this context, my role as a religious leader was not to be some lone prophet out front, but rather to be a gathering agent within this mixed group, sponsoring alliances that would leverage the power and authority that business and political leaders may have in larger measure than do we religious leaders in contemporary society.

Working interdependently, we do not have less power, but more, and of a different sort. From this new perspective, power becomes a measure of the healthy functioning of the group, the degree of utilization of its varied gifts, and the marshalling of its collective insight into complex issues.

Intriguing Parallels

Two leadership theorists, Sally Helgesen and Jean Lipman-Blumen, offer insight into these discoveries. Helgesen, whose organizational theory of the "web of inclusion" was introduced in chapter 3, characterizes this mode as "feminine" because it emphasizes inclusive relationship and responsible participation:

> What I came up with always bore a literal, architectural resemblance to a spider's web. . . . I added the term "inclusion" to the notion of the web because the women who led the organizations labored continually to bring everyone at every point closer to the center — to tighten ties, provide increased exposure and greater participation.[24]

Lipman-Blumen calls this emphasis "connective." asserting that this relational mode is an appropriate response to a world challenged by individualism and diversity. She acknowledges that women, in particular, exercise relational roles in our society and serve as links between the private and public domains:

> The human linkages created through connective leadership ultimately build a sense of community, where respect for individual differences and responsibility toward the group go hand in hand. Exploiting the strengths of diversity, connective leaders build community and entrust a wide range of people, many unlike themselves, to share the burdens of leadership.[25]

She too notes that this type of leader knows that leadership can be offered from a variety of positions.

> Connective leaders perceive that interdependence means relationships of all kinds, among people, among organizations, and among nations. They therefore use relationships in multiple ways to accomplish their leadership tasks. They feel equally comfortable as members of the team, as behind-the-scenes helpers, or as facilitators and mentors.[26]

Finally, Lipman-Blumen also speaks of the differences in architectural terms, saying that connective leaders do not focus on vertical relationships and hierarchies, but instead on "egalitarian and horizontal structures, with no one giving orders and no one snapping to attention."[27]

By putting women at the center of the web, Helgesen acknowledges that they have some special authority in the web's design; its purpose, however, is to pull others closer to the decision-making. The image of the web is helpful in thinking about the women I spoke with because it honors their entrepreneurial initiative while acknowledging their reliance on the ideas and energies of others. The web has a weaver, yes. But the center cannot be seen apart from its radiating arms and connecting strands.

Embodiment as Integrity

Along with this preference for a leadership architecture which relies on interdependent collaborative relationships, my conversations with women leaders revealed another area of remarkable consensus: the insistence that leaders have integrity. Some had first seen it in role models and mentors who had been important to them. One, for instance, referred to the compelling "incarnational" quality of Martin Luther King Jr. In general, the women defined integrity as a close coherence between word and action, the ability to consistently live their beliefs. For them, simply pointing the way forward is not enough. As one woman put it: "It's not about exhorters, not people saying, 'Hey, why don't all of you go do that.'" Instead, it is a question of embodiment — actually behaving a vision of a better way.

For instance, when Ruth Messinger reflected with me about how she gathered and sustained support throughout her twenty years in politics, she credited her ability to live her progressive values:

> I knew a lot of people in a lot of different groups and movements, and so they knew my politics were very grassroots-focused and my style was inclusive and consultative, and I was smart. I think even before I took office, there were people who had a sense that I would really live a commitment to diversity instead of just talk about it.

Another woman told me, "Integrity is when the outer and inner person are one." When a person of integrity is present, there are no mixed signals, no static or dissonance. Leading with integrity is seen by these women as a means of activating a group, as if by the power of resonance. "A leader is someone who embodies what they see and empowers others to do the same."

As we saw in chapter 2, the women's conviction about actualizing a vision extends to their organizations as well. Alicia Del Tufo, founder of several organizations which seek to reduce domestic violence, told me:

> I've always wanted my efforts to change the world to have a kind of integrity. Like, if I was interested in doing something that was going to help clients "live better lives," I had this idea that the structure that provided that help should also be a place that was nurturing and a positive environment for those who work there. So I had this very organic idea. And then the women who I worked with at Sanctuary were very invested in the concept of its being this integrated place where you tried to be a person who had nonviolent, nonabusive ways of interacting with your co-workers as well as with the people who came for help. So it was a modeling kind of thing.

In chapter 7 we will see how this emphasis on walking the talk fits into an overall pattern of wanting to lead a "seamless" life. This insistence on incarnation — putting flesh on one's principles — also echoes the discussion of the one-on-one systemic dance in chapter 3. There we saw that being connected to actual people in need brings the abstraction of public issues alive for these leaders. Here, their emphasis on actually modeling new behaviors is another form of grounding — providing glimpses, both personal and organizational, of what alternatives look like.

In my mind, this insistence on embodied values is akin to the women's preference for leadership from within the group. A vision for change is not a finger pointing ahead of us all, but a body and a collective, living it along. That is, these women insist that their values not be out in front of their ability to enact them. They don't let their dreams get ahead of them, so to speak. Instead, they wait for them to fill from beneath and within. What counts is what the body can live. Just so, leading from within or behind the group entails proceeding at a pace the group can sponsor and sustain.

In fact, many of the women's definitions of leadership stressed the importance of activating and tapping the power of the group. Lee Hancock, who earlier offered the orchestra conductor image, elaborated it this way:

> I think a leader is someone who can listen, who can call forth gifts from people which they need to exercise but may not know that they have. A leader is someone who can create a team, who can help people to feel good about themselves, and who can transform what can be very mundane and ordinary work into something that's fun and meaningful. I think a good leader endows collective effort with meaning.

This sense of meaningful effort, I believe, arises out of the confluence of people's varied gifts being well used on behalf of a worthy vision of a better way to live. That is, the content of the vision or dream matters. Worthy content is what allows people to feel that their participation makes a meaningful contribution. Here is where effective leadership becomes what I consider to be faithful leadership. As we have discovered in earlier chapters, many of these women were first drawn into the work because of an intuition or moral conviction about what was right — that children need shelter and food, that people with HIV/AIDS need nourishing food whether they can cook it or not, that violence against women must be stopped. They chose to step into uncharted territory, fueled by a desire to incarnate an image of how the world could be. From behind, within, and beneath the problems, and in the company of trusted others, they brought a new kind of leverage to bear. Now, daring to behave what they believe, they have begun to bring bits of the could-be world to life.

In the next chapter we will explore questions of meaning further, as we look at how these women feel about themselves as religious leaders. As we shall see, there is ambivalence about claiming the title of religious leader as well, and less consensus about how it might be redefined.

Chapter 5

BEARING RELIGION

"I like the breaking of the glass at the end of the ceremony," said the young man describing the only nod to his Jewish heritage that he wished to include in the wedding service to his bride, the offspring of a Lutheran mother and a Greek Orthodox father. What the groom did not comprehend is that this ritual did not just appear ex nihilo for his enjoyment, but has, like all religious rituals, an historical, theological, and sociological context. Rituals *become* rituals because they are capable of carrying the numinous; as symbols of a host of meanings and associations, some of which we may only partially grasp, they have the power to reconnect us with what we hold sacred. But without regular practice, meditation upon their mysteries, and nurture in a community of faith, all rituals — including hymns, images, and sacred stories — lose their numinous charge and become merely hollow forms.

Do I sound like some crazed apologist for an antiquated and irrelevant past?

That's not how I see it. As a religious leader, I consider it one of my primary responsibilities to continually ask, "Where is God in this?" — whether "this" is a wedding, a conference on the Middle East, or a meeting with a potential donor. These days, almost every couple I marry claims to be "spiritual" but not religious, and we do a dance of accommodation to make the experience authentic enough for each of us. I try with good humor to use the opportunity to raise at least some of the questions of meaning, faith, family, and responsibility toward the world which bear upon our collective future — deeper matters that will surely resurface once the wedding frenzy dissipates.

Oftentimes this involves an act of archeology on my part. I need to help people dig into the imagery at hand to reconnect with buried meanings which are vibrant still. Take, for instance, the breaking of the glass. The rabbis report that the ritual dates back to the time after the destruction of the Temple in 70 CE, a time of despair and exile for the Jewish people. The legends tell of a rabbi who threw a glass to the floor, berating the guests at his son's wedding for celebrating and dancing in the face of devastation and death. Thus, the breaking glass catches that moment when celebration and mourning touch, and suggests that each must be experienced in light of the other — that in all moments of deep grief there is the glimmer of hope, and behind all experience of human exile, estrangement, and desolation there stands the everlasting promise of God's presence and love. The Christian parallel to this is the symbol of resurrection: the Easter celebration following upon the events of Good Friday.

There is yet another layer here. In many respects, weddings celebrate personal relationship — the joining of the bride and groom and their extended families. But the Temple was the embodiment of Yahweh's special relationship with the whole of the Jewish people. Thus the breaking of the glass is an insistence that a broader field of relationships be tended — self and spouse, yes, but also self and God, as well as self and God's people. In the Jewish tradition, this nexus of connections is principally tended through the practice of *tikkun olam*, repairing the world.

Did the young groom know this when he asked for the ritual of the glass, or was he simply drawn to its dramatic flair? Or did he subscribe to the popular understanding which, ironically, emphasizes not the careful tending of relationship but the couple's independence from their families of origin to create something new? I knew the groom to be a man of sensitivity and compassion. In his early twenties he had moved in with his grandmother to care for her until her death. As a minister, thinking of the inevitable hard times ahead, I wanted him to know — for his sake and for the world's sake — that his compassion for his grandmother was mirrored in God's compassion for human beings. I wanted to reveal to him that in Hebrew *compassion* and *womb* share the same root, and that both are associated with God's very being — that compassion is a life-giving creative act. I wanted him to discover that beneath his seemingly casual preference for the glass lay a living rhizome, the root system of spiritual food for a lifetime. And I wanted to offer some analogous sustenance to the bride, who had expressed no particular connection with the traditions of either of her parents. They had come to a minister, a religious leader, to marry them. Something in them wanted "more" than a justice of the peace. How could I meet this hunger while honoring their precise mix of secularism, ethnic heritage, and "not religious" faith?

◆ ◆ ◆

This vignette is a simple reminder of the complexity of feelings human beings harbor toward the subject and experience of religion. They are at once repelled and attracted, unsure about publicly associating themselves with it. Many have had their trust betrayed by the failings of religious professionals and communities. Others are rightfully appalled by the record of history wherein, in the name of religion, acts of negligence, zeal, and misguided vision have resulted in the persecution, wounding, or death of millions of people. It can be tempting to argue that society would be better off without organized religion. And yet . . . and yet. There is a force stronger than mere nostalgia which makes people hunger still for the other face of religion, the one that orients us within life's mysteries and struggles. Even if there is no way back to the faith stance of our childhood, might there be a way forward? Are there ways for religion still to play a vital role in our public deliberation about the things that matter most?

Moving toward a Broader Definition

It was this complicated phenomenon that I wanted to probe as I approached the matter of religion with the leaders I interviewed. I asked them such questions as: Was religion a part of your family life growing up? How do characterize your current relationship with organized religion? Can you describe your current spirituality or faith stance and comment on whether it influences your work? Do you see yourself as a religious leader? What images, symbols, or stories guide and empower you? What are your basic views about how society works best?

I hoped, of course, to get a clearer picture of what it means to be a public religious leader in a pluralistic society. I had chosen to speak with these women because I felt they were already doing this. But I quickly learned that I was making an assumption that even some of these innovative leaders did not at first share. I define ministry and religious leadership broadly. In my view, we must move beyond the narrower notion of ordained clergy, usually men, leading congregations. In fact, an increasing number of women serve in this role and this remains a vital means of bearing religion forward. Yet I was drawn to the women in this book precisely because, by working largely outside the walls of churches and mosques and synagogues, they are taking religion public again.

What do I mean by that? It is not that they are out there proselytizing, seeking converts to a particular ideology. I mean that they are bringing the insights of faith to bear on public issues. They are acting in the wider world upon their beliefs about inclusive justice and interdependent relationship. In public issue debates, they are the ones raising the ethical and moral questions. Though they may not always use explicitly religious language, they approach problems from a religious perspective — that is, with a sensitivity to questions of meaning, human purpose, and the wonder and dignity of all of life. That is what I consider to be religious leadership.

A Complex Love-Hate Relationship

I was surprised to find that several of the women I interviewed, including some ordained clergy, are ambivalent about the designation "religious leader." Even more so than with the term "leader," they seem affected by the undertow of the traditional definition. But a too-narrow definition is only one piece of the puzzle. There are other factors at play. Some of the women clearly want to distance themselves from public assumptions about religious leaders — an act of resistance against forms of behavior toward which they are sharply critical. Others simply feel they can be more effective in their given contexts if they do not emphasize their religious groundings (a strategy which I shall return to in chapter 6 concerning the use of religious language). Some wrestle with whether voicing their own evolving faith stance, which they know to be at odds with their denominations in significant areas, will be recognized as "leadership."

My other questions about religion also evoked multivalent responses. In chapter 8 we will look more closely at the question of early influences. Many of these women had stories to tell about being betrayed by organized religion. As we shall see, that is an ongoing struggle. Religion continues to fail their expectations. Yet that is only part of their experience. Most also had vivid stories of religion's power to inform and sustain their work. A number confessed to having a kind of love-hate relationship with organized religion. Instead of discarding it as irrelevant or potentially too destructive, they have chosen to hold on and dig deeper. To a significant degree, it is religion's very failure to fulfill its own promise to them which motivates them to bear with it a while longer. They know what a force for good it can be, and seek to embody that in their lives and work. As we shall see, bearing religion forward in this way, in the dual sense of consciously holding both its devastating shortcomings and its undeniable promise, paradoxically entails a willingness to loosen one's grip on traditional images so that they are free to transform and reveal fresh insight.

To better appreciate this complex stance toward religion, let's listen to the women themselves as they describe their love-hate relationship with their traditions as well as some ways of working with imagery which they are finding fruitful. First, their critiques.

Critiques and Betrayals

The Candles in the Cathedrals Have Gone Out

With fierce energy, Gretchen Buchenholz, whom we met in chapter 1, told me that she did not consider herself a religious leader. It was not that religious imagery failed to resonate for her, nor that she was unwilling to be a moral voice. It was that she wanted to make a clear distinction between herself and those who professed to be religious but did not speak out or act. Recall her sharp indictment: "The public argument has squeezed out the voices of faith. It has swallowed up and silenced, to a great degree, the impulse we all have to care for the least of us. All of our traditions tell us that we should do that, and that we're diminished if we don't. Horrible things have happened, horrible things . . . and the church has participated by its silence and inaction." She then used the haunting metaphor "the candles in all the cathedrals are out" to capture the failure of religious institutions and leaders to kindle the light of hope.

Barbara Dobkin, philanthropist and activist, founded Ma'yan, the Jewish Women's Project, currently at the Jewish Community Center on Manhattan's Upper West Side. She told me she started her organization because she feels Jewish synagogues and agencies, dominated by male authority, are reluctant to reform internally let alone enact feminist religious values in the outside world. "I think my need to start Ma'yan . . . was that I couldn't find a place for myself religiously," she mused. She is not alone. Programs offered by Ma'yan are attended by hundreds of women who are looking for a different religious expression ritually, and who want to enact progressive religious values in the public realm as well as in the Jewish world to which they belong.

Several of the women I spoke with felt frustrated with how denominational squabbling saps so much energy that might be directed elsewhere. Religious institutions have subdivided into special interest groups that lobby narrowly along ideological lines, instead of working together toward a larger shared vision. Battles over issues of sexuality, as critical as those are because lives are at stake, have absorbed mainline Protestants, especially Presbyterians, Episcopalians, and Methodists, of late. As one of the women put it: "I think at this point they all have to give up their particular swords — the abortion sword, the death penalty sword, the ordination swords — and focus on the common ground."

An area of common ground, several suggested, is the growing disparity between the rich and the poor, both within this country, and between the United States and the rest of the world. As these women see it, when faith communities do not use the moral influence they have, they actually help perpetuate the problem.

> I think that if one truly lives out one's faith — be it Christianity, be it Islam, be it Judaism — there is the obligation to share. Unfortunately, I feel that our churches and other religious institutions are not addressing that. We have churches at the top not doing all they should be doing, so they reinforce the status quo.

Annie Bovian, an ordained minister who is working to transform the criminal justice system, took this critique a step further, charging that churches themselves have been corrupted by their own desire for wealth.

I have been very disappointed by the way the church has reacted to the needs of the poor. In New York, I find that churches for the most part are interested in real estate more so than caring for people who are in need. You find that churches do not get involved with people in prison — and I mean on a day-to-day basis, not just Easter. You know why? Because people in prison can't tithe.

More broadly, Sister Helen Prejean, a lifelong nun, warned that organized religion is always in danger of losing its connection to its core purpose.

Religion can put you into a nice, comfortable, private club where you come together once a week, you're made to feel comfortable, and you sing hymns that make you feel very close to each other and close to God. But that's got nothing to do with igniting the passion to get out there and be in solidarity with the suffering and the hurting people of society, as in the tradition of the prophets and in Jesus himself.

As these excerpts suggest, the women I interviewed saw the church and other organized religious bodies as being absorbed with maintenance, survival, and internal conflicts over status and identity rather than with their deeper vocation of inspiring people to act on behalf of justice and social transformation. In short, the critique is that many who head religious organizations are behaving as managers of institutional resources rather than as authentic leaders.

I'm Not That Kind of Religious Leader

In protest, the women I interviewed are in effect saying, "I'm not that kind of religious leader." And their desire to distance themselves is at least twofold. On the one hand, these progressive women leaders are frustrated with many of the positions taken by the Religious Right.

But they also fault liberals for being silent so long. They are looking for a third place to stand as religious leaders which is neither this nor that. Almost without realizing it, they have been busy creating that very ground to stand on, creating, that is, a more authentic form of religious leadership. Ironically, though, they are not confident about calling it that.

Barbara Dobkin, for instance, contends with the shifting politics of Judaism in which Orthodox Jews seek to define who is in and who is out. She is aware that her feminist views and evolving understanding of the Divine represent significant breaks with tradition and orthodoxy. Noting that growing conservatism within Judaism now seems to leave little room for those who are more liberal in their faith, she explains, "I just have a hard time with my religion and how that gets defined." As the embodiment of an alternative definition, she must constantly hold her own.

Annie Bovian also contends with the fact that her definition of religious leadership differs from that of the people she serves. Ordained in the United Church of Christ, she directs a court advocacy program. When she works with women prisoners, she does introduce herself as a minister but then is careful to intercept and reinterpret preconceptions they might have. "I don't want them to get the idea that God is going to take them out of this. It doesn't happen that way." Rather than allowing them to blame the system or expect magical solutions, she uses biblical stories and metaphors to help the women focus on the difficult behavioral shifts they need to make. Yet she is also nurturing. So many of them, she tells me, convey to her an unspoken question: "no matter what I've done, do you still think I'm worth anything?" Her answer is unwavering: "Yes, you are one of God's children."

Other women I spoke with found the narrower definition of religious leadership neither fitting nor strategic. Laura Jervis, an ordained Presbyterian minister and founder of West Side Federation for Senior Housing, spoke of the complexities of identifying herself as a religious leader in a diverse urban area. Especially in the initial stages of her work, because she had the vision of building a multifaith constituency of outreach and support for poor elderly, she deliberately "put my role as a minister toward the back of things — really diminished my identity." She did not want to be perceived as pushing a religious approach on persons who were avowed secular humanists, nor a sectarian agenda on people of other faith traditions (such as Jews on her board of directors).

She was also finding that her own religious convictions were in flux. When we spoke, she acknowledged being alienated by what is happening in the national Presbyterian Church around women, and especially around barring lesbians and gays from ordination as ministers. Though she still leads worship as a Presbyterian minister and fulfills duties in the governance of the church at the local level, her disaffection runs deep. "I don't feel like I'm ordained in the Presbyterian Church; I don't feel that at all." She now regularly incorporates other religious experiences into her practice, like receiving communion at a Catholic Mass and being an honorary member of a neighborhood synagogue.

Though these women are hampered by the narrow definition of religious leadership, they are determined to do their part to craft a more fitting one. This they do not view as an abstract exercise, but as a challenge to get out and embody a new way of being. As one put it:

> It's the church's responsibility not to sit on the sidelines and let the far Right define who we are, but to work with people, to say that our very humanity is at stake here, and to get the church to move more and more from private spaces to public life so that public life can affect the political arena.

Where does such determination come from? In short, from a potent mix of anger and hope.

Blowing on Coals from the Margins

Angry women are often dismissed as shrill, strident, hysterical. My mother, now in her eighties, still recalls that when she showed her anger as a small child of three or four, her father threw a bucket of cold well water on her — a pretty clear signal to put the fire out! But these women leaders have ignored that strong cultural message. They are actually using their outrage at the church's failings as fuel to relight the candles in the cathedrals. Alchemists that they are, they know the power of heat to transform even the most recalcitrant material. They also have learned the necessity of regulating the heat, an awareness they share with a long line of activists.

Miles Horton, founder of the Highlander school where Martin Luther King Jr. and many others learned to wield the tools of social change, considered rage an appropriate response to the ongoing presence of injustice. He said, "If you ever get to the place where injustice doesn't bother you, you're dead."[28] But changing entrenched habits and systems requires effort applied over the long haul. For this he recommended a transmuted rage:

> It wasn't easy to get to a place where I didn't scare people away with my determination to change a system that I believed to be unjust, but I tried my best to avoid sounding like an evangelist. I had to turn my anger into a slow-burning fire, instead of a consuming fire.... It keeps you going, but you subdue it, because you don't want to be destroyed by it.[29]

In addition to turning their outrage into fuel, the women I interviewed are honoring another of their instincts by turning it into a deliberate strategy. They are taking their urge to distance themselves from organized religion and making it into a choice to work from the margins. This placement, they feel, gives them the freedom to address public issues more directly, as well as to experiment with and model

alternatives to what both organized religion and government are offering. These women are not simply gadflies or lone prophets railing
at the system from afar, they are engaged activists who feel that for
now, their best means of leveraging change is from positions at the
edges of institutions and systems rather than as the designated leaders
within them.

Remaining Rooted in Religion

But why do they choose to stay in this love-hate relationship at all?
Given all the critiques they have and the resistance to change which
many institutions exhibit, why bother? Why not cut all ties with organized religion and be "spiritual, not religious?" Why not be a secular
social worker, simply doing good and leaving God and faith out of it?
Ironically or predictably, depending on where you stand, the answer
comes from the faith traditions themselves. Yes, these women have
been betrayed by organized religion. But as they explained it to me,
that very sense of betrayal arises from the fact that each has also already
experienced something of the vision and promise of faith. Their outrage is the reaction of those who know better, and that very wisdom,
in large measure, has been conveyed to them through religious imagery
and practice. Thus, in varying ways, they are choosing to bridge the gap
between betrayal and promise, hoping to help redirect religion toward
its own professed vocation. They "blow on the coals of its heart" (to
paraphrase Archibald MacLeish) because they believe that heart is alive
and worth saving. Lee Hancock expressed her motivations this way:

> I'm a bridge person. I'm a person who believes that the church
> exists to serve the world. I'm not a person who's willing to give
> up the church and just go out into the world and be an activist
> on health care issues. Because I think that whatever religion is
> about — and that is to say healing and wisdom and education and

activism and justice — that all of those more substantial virtues and goals aren't really raised up any other place. So I will continue to be rooted in religion, even though the church is currently far too small and far too self-involved.

Citing historical examples, another voiced a similar hope that religious institutions will soon discover "the better angels of their nature":

> I know that the church can make a huge difference. I've experienced it. I've seen when the church decided there shouldn't be a war in Vietnam, that the civil rights laws needed to be passed, that apartheid was evil and had to end, that the Contras needed to be challenged. I mean, you can just go through the litany of times in which the church came together and said: "This we are going to stop."

Remember that even Gretchen, so adamant about not being a religious leader, predicts that the necessary change will occur. "I think we've lost our moral bearings for the time being," she says, "but I don't think they're lost for good. We just need to trim the sails here. If anything feels like my mission, that's it."

Conviction like this reminds me of what I had come to know as a child in the figure of Dietrich Bonhoeffer, Lutheran pastor and leader in the Resistance movement against Hitler. These women, I feel, are expressing the underlying motives of resistance faith: outrage at injustice, critique of the status quo, and a desire to reclaim the radical or root understandings of religious teachings. Because such people still find sustenance in their faith traditions, I think of them not as iconoclasts but as radical traditionalists. That is, they value tradition but recognize the need to dig deeper, to push beyond or beneath current understandings and practices in order to reestablish connection with the core. They realize that often what is needed is a fresh way of connecting these core messages with contemporary public issues.

Religious "truths" seem enduring and timeless, but they are not carved in stone. They are but partial renderings of a mystery and wholeness we cannot fully absorb. We hold them sacred for what they do convey, but we must not hold them so tightly that they cannot continue to transmute before our eyes. They are more like the rhizomes of a living root system extending beneath, within, and beyond us. As living things, they are growing and evolving, perhaps at glacial speed, but inexorably nonetheless. We need to give them room to breathe. If we hold them gently and explore them open-heartedly and almost playfully, tilting them this way and that, we will find that they have dimensions we have not appreciated before — that they have even more to say than we have yet imagined.

Rediscovering the Radical Essence

It was when I asked each woman I interviewed if and how her faith connected with her public work that I learned about the dialogues they were having with their traditions' root systems. They felt that the core messages and mandates of their traditions clearly point to transforming the public arena. They emphasized images of compassion and justice rather than power or judgment. Connie Baugh told me:

> I think the essential connection between religion and public life is "Love one another as I have loved you." This is the mandate from Jesus: to do justice — not simply avoid evil, but resist evil. That's the religious mandate. The wounded person on the side of the road, you know. The impetus for compassion, to me, comes out of religion — finding God in the face of each other, especially those who are hurting the most. There's a long tradition that says that's where God is found, so to me that's the natural link.

Connie is saying that avoiding evil is not enough. An active resistance of it is required, and that occurs in the practice of compassion. We can also see here that the way one thinks about the nature of God is linked to the vision one holds for society at its best. Taken seriously and truly enacted, the conviction that there is that of God in everyone has radical implications for the behavior of individuals as well as social systems.

Like Connie, Muslim scholar and activist Riffat Hassan is convinced that some form of social action is mandated by her faith:

> You know, it's almost like a form of worship for me, because I think that striving for social justice, striving for the rights of the disadvantaged is very fundamental to all our traditions. All of our traditions talk about the care of the widow, the orphan, the person discriminated against. For me, personally, this is religious work, although there are people who are joining this effort who are not religious, who are doing it because they are human rights activists. And that's fine, but I think that many people who are religious are also beginning to see that there is so much more to being religious than simply leading a good life within your own sphere of activities, but that you have to go out into the world and do something to change it. That's the imperative we have to follow.

Mychal Springer told me that growing up in the Reform movement in Judaism gave her clear sense of religion's link with public life even as a teenager:

> The Reform movement is very focused on making the world a better place, so especially the old Union Prayerbook was very focused on righteousness, acts of loving kindness. And that would be just drilled into you. There's a part of the service that's silent prayer, and my only prayer was, "God help me to help other people."

Activism as worship and prayer. Activism as the natural outcome of taking seriously the essential messages of our faith traditions. Treat everyone, publicly and privately, as if they are bearing a bit of God. That is what these women were telling me.

Becoming God's Body

They were also telling me that certain images about the nature of God, or the character of the God-energy, guided their chosen forms of activism. Sister Helen Prejean, for example, finds that she gains the necessary courage for her work by allowing herself to be moved by a great flowing energy:

> What motivates me, what moves me, is my faith, at the core of action. My prayer is a whole way of aligning myself with the energy of God. To me, the big image is energy, movement, a stream. So you put your little boat in the stream. And when you're in the stream and God's love is flowing through you, you can be bold. You just say, for example, "the death penalty is wrong, people are suffering, there's great injustice — I will take it on. I will work for its abolition."

Mychal Springer shared an image of God that she finds critical for keeping herself engaged and centered:

> In the Ten Commandments, God says that God is an *el kanah,* which is often translated as a jealous God, but actually means an impassioned God, a God of all feelings. So, I understand myself as being created in God's image, as being a woman of passion, an impassioned person. That image really guides me and keeps me from jumping into a head place. It's through those passions that I connect with people and have access to what's sacred in them. I think it helps us actually be in the work together. So, learning to be embodied in that way has been huge.

An image of God as encompassing all passions is very freeing, particularly for women. It provides a theological understanding of anger, for example, as a passion that can be channeled for beneficial purposes. And, as Mychal notes, it balances a heady approach.

Henna Hahn's outreach to abused Korean women is shaped by her own wrestling with traditional understandings of God as high and mighty. Drawing on the Korean notion of the mother's house as a nurturing haven even for adult women (see chapter 2), she had imagined God as the compassionate mother of the Rainbow Center and she and the clients as the sisters. Following the implications of the image, she found herself with a whole new notion of power:

> What is the almightiness of God? Now I can realize God's almightiness is lowness, not highness. Before this ministry, I thought that God is big and strong and powerful. Highness, authority — something like that. Now I think I cannot bend much lower, but God can bend because God is almighty. That's what I want to try to do myself, not to be strong and powerful — the leader — I'm not that person. I want to be more powerless, bending.

As Henna and I spoke further, I learned that this view of God derives from Minjung theology — a theology of Korean Christians who were trying to fight the repressive activities of the South Korean government. It is a theology which emphasizes that God favors the poor and that Jesus the suffering Messiah is God's embodiment among them. Might, as this image has it, is not about height, but about bending and connection. It is the passion to reach and embrace the lowliest who, come to find out, feel more like our sisters than our subjects.

Lee Hancock's image of God has sustained her work in healing communities affected by HIV/AIDS. It was given to her by her mentor and has been an orienting focus for years as she struggles with a chronic health condition of her own and seeks healing for others:

He came to me when I was so sick. And he quoted Alfred North Whitehead and he said: "God is a fellow sufferer who understands." That gave me a process, an entry into reworking my theology. Now I really understood God as the fellow sufferer, God as the compassionate presence, God not as the grand puppeteer pulling the strings, but God as the compassionate heart in the middle of suffering. So, all my ministry is lived out of that vision.

I wish I could convey to you the shift that occurred in the interviews when these women started talking about these core images. Though many had been reluctant at the outset to call themselves religious leaders, when I asked how their work in the world connected with the life of Spirit, all of a sudden the interviews were teeming with images and metaphors, baseline theologies, inner compasses that guided and motivated them, sometimes over the course of decades of really difficult work. And the images did not always come from official religious sources. Ginny Thornburgh, for instance, talked excitedly about the memory of standing with her father, who was in the steamship business, and watching bulging nets of cargo swing safely from the ships to the dock. Whenever the stresses of her work threaten to overwhelm her, she thinks of God as "this net holding me, and holding me even if I am straining, even if the load is heavy or awkward."

What struck me was that in citing the religious influences that informed their work for justice, these leaders did not reference doctrine or sectarian dogma, but deeper and broader images that have resonance in Christianity, Judaism, Islam, and other traditions: God as Mother, Creative force, God of relation, God as fellow sufferer. We can see that even though most of these women are not clergy serving in churches, their images of God have shaped the characteristics and dynamics of the organizations they have created and the way they behave within them. Thus, an essential piece of how they are bearing religion forward in these times is that they are embodying these previously underemphasized aspects of wholeness. The holding environments which are their organizations are, as it were, bearing more of God's body into our world.

Making Space for Religious Sensibilities

Another critical way in which these women serve as bearers of religion is by creating space in public settings for particular values and types of conversations. I think of it as having an almost architectural quality to it. It literally creates an opening that was not there before and transforms it into sacred space by virtue of the quality of connection that begins to happen there. The women do this by having the presence to press the pause button in the midst of a given workplace dynamic and then prompt reflection from an ethical or religious perspective. Usually, this involves introducing values and ways of thinking which challenge prevailing norms. Here are some examples.

As we saw earlier, Laura Jervis, director of West Side Federation for Senior Housing, had been scrupulous early in her career to keep her role as minister in the background. Yet she noted that as she has matured, she is finding that she compartmentalizes those roles less and less. She now considers WSFSH "more and more as my parish" with herself as "the spiritual center" (though she shied from the potential grandiosity of the image). This freedom to blend a minister's sensibilities with those of a CEO has come partly from within and partly out of the trust she has built with her staff over several decades.

When I asked her to elaborate on how she lived out this blended role, she first cited traditional ministerial duties like performing burial rituals for residents or "setting the tone" for end-of-life decisions. Then she recalled a specific incident that to me reveals her deep conviction about the primacy of relationships and demonstrates moral leadership in a more innovative sense.

A resident of one of her buildings had become unstable and had slashed a passerby with a box cutter. The staff was very upset by this. Uppermost in their minds was fear of a lawsuit. Laura gathered them together and offered an entirely different framework. She explained that she felt that the lawsuit would not be an issue if the relationships were cared for properly. She had already called the victim to express her concern and had also reached out to the resident. "It totally changed the mood [in the staff meeting]," Laura recounted, "and I could tell that what I said is what in their hearts they wanted to hear, but they couldn't believe that I would take that approach."

When I asked her why she was not more concerned about a lawsuit, she said, "Because I knew that the primary issues were relational issues: showing concern for these two people who were so affected by the moment, and how to connect them. That was the primary thing." This kind of response might have lawyers cringing, but Laura had the presence to step into a tense situation and refocus everyone's attention. She modeled a different kind of moral leadership by preferencing the relational over the litigious. And that single incident may have created a more permanent opening for a different way of proceeding. As Laura told me, "There's been kind of a perceptual shift in terms of my relationship with that staff and what they're thinking about. They've asked me to come to their staff retreat and talk about the realm of ethics — to offer some guidance there rather than address the nitty-gritty work that they do every day."

Healing is a major focus for many of the women leaders, whether it is directed at individuals, organizations, or the wider community and culture. Again I saw the "making space" dynamic at work. When she was a hospital chaplain Mychal Springer had a vision of reshaping the whole hospital environment by introducing a new paradigm of healing that promotes the interconnectedness of body, mind, and spirit. This involved not only making chaplains an integral part of the care-giving teams, it meant creating occasions to honor and care for the pastoral needs of the entire staff.

As we saw in chapter 2, Mychal has diagnosed us as a "sunshine society" more able to talk about triumph than pain. But because she stayed so close to pain and suffering in the hospital culture, she understood that acknowledging the shadow actually builds stronger communities where people can be in relationship with each other. As a bearer of religion, she had the presence to say, "I know we're hurting, and let's make room for that."

In addition to making space for talk about suffering, Mychal told me she regularly creates opportunities for people to talk about how their faith connects with the other parts of their lives, thus helping to heal the split between belief and action.

> My experience is that most people don't really talk about their beliefs, and how they really look at the world in terms of their beliefs. So, probably the most radical way I lead religiously is that I give the message that articulating what we believe and working toward living it out is important.

Like Mychal and Laura, Jan Orr-Harter identified one of her roles as counteracting compartmentalized thinking and fostering religious reflection on a full range of human activities.

> When something amazing had happened, like being at a gay pride march or traveling to DC to protest a policy, I'd ask people afterward, "Where in the situation did you see God?" I think it's an important way to help people to reflect on their lives. And that's pretty much how the liberation praxis works, with action and reflection groups in South America. I always thought we were kind of building a North American version of that.

In an increasingly hurried world, Jan insists that reflection is the essential partner to action. She, Mychal, and Laura bear religion forward by being the kind of presence who will ensure that public issues be viewed with a frame of reference that is at once wider and more intimate — one which asks us to consider where Spirit is at work in us at this very moment of conflict and struggle; one which asks us to focus more on how we are intertwined in each other's destinies; one which upholds the conviction that thoughtful, caring dialogue about our pain and differences will move us toward a greater realization of our wholeness, both individually and collectively.

By making space for moral and spiritual questions in public, these women leaders are actually inviting religion back to its rightful place at the table of public debate. But I cannot stress enough that there are significant acts of translation and reinterpretation involved in doing this effectively and appropriately in a multifaith context. Being a bearer of religion in today's world means developing some key competencies: channeling anger, holding to a relationship ethic, being a centered presence in sometimes chaotic situations, digging deeper into the root system of organized religion, being able to make appropriate and insightful connections between religious imagery and current events, and, as Riffat Hassan described it to me, just generally offering "better religious arguments" than we have heard of late.

Learning to Make
Better Religious Arguments

Riffat Hassan began making the connection between Islam, feminism, and human rights over twenty-five years ago when she became faculty advisor to a Muslim student group at Oklahoma State University. The Arab Muslims from the Gulf States and Saudi Arabia were "extremely patriarchal in their mind-set" and didn't let women into their membership. Yet since it was customary for the advisor to speak at their annual seminar, they did invite Riffat to speak briefly on women in Islam, apparently assuming that this was the only topic about which she would be qualified to speak. Riffat seized the moment as an opportunity to be a different sort of presence in the room.

> Having come across hundreds of writings on women in Islam, books, brochures, articles, etcetera, virtually all of them written by men who were defining what women were and what their duties were as good Muslim women, as wives and mothers, I had a pretty good idea as to what these students were expecting me to say, and I knew I wasn't going to say that.
>
> Anyhow, I accepted that invitation for two reasons. One was that I thought that at least they'll hear a different perspective. And the second one was I was really disturbed by the fact that they did not allow women anywhere near the seminar. They believed that if a Muslim man hears the voice of a woman who is not related to him, that it puts his soul in jeopardy, so I said, "Well, that's good, at least they'll have to hear my voice."

The invitation was a catalytic moment for Riffat. It prompted her to dive deeper into the discrepancy between what the Koran itself affirmed about the rights of women and what was happening to Muslim women in Muslim countries. Not simply a scholarly exercise, this was an issue which reverberated with her personal life.

> I began to see how many things had happened to me because I had been born female in a Muslim society. I started to feel very very angry, and I think in a way that anger has stayed with me all these years, because I feel that the teachings are misunderstood or manipulated in such a way as to be disadvantageous to women.

In the years following her invitation to speak, she continued her excavation toward a pre-patriarchal understanding of the Koran and wrote numerous articles offering her reinterpretations. During the 1980s, when she began to spend several years at a time in her homeland of Pakistan, she realized that women were the primary targets for control and punishment as that society underwent a conservative wave of Islamization. Women activists who knew of her research began coming to her in the mid-eighties asking for her help to challenge the repressive laws that were being exercised in the name of Islam.

Riffat began a deeper investigation asking why in a progressive Muslim country like Pakistan these laws were being promulgated — and, more profoundly still, why women's inferiority to men was considered a bedrock principle in the culture. Studying all of the creation stories in the Koran, she concluded that none differentiated hierarchically between men and women. Instead, they simply spoke of human beings having been created equally in the eyes of God. But in the Haddith or oral interpretative tradition which followed, there began to grow up the story of woman's creation from the rib of man. This image of a woman's life being derivative of a man's entered into Islamic tradition and the repressive forms of culture relied on this interpretation rather than the original text.

Although women activists she knew sometimes became impatient with her scholarship and pressed for more political action, Riffat insisted that if you are on a train that gets off on the wrong track, "you have to go back to the point at which you were derailed to get back on track.... It is very important for women to recreate this whole journey." For Riffat, the theological issue lies at the heart of the political one: if man and woman are equal in the eyes of God, then inequality is not the will of God.

The only way that Muslim women can counter the situation is by developing better religious arguments. You cannot defeat a religious argument only by means of political action. Some people think they can. I don't happen to agree with that. I think that they will have to be countered by better religious arguments . . . to show what is being done to women in the name of Islam is not Islam, but a misinterpretation of Islam.

Having done her homework, she took her case into the public realm. Relying largely on the connective power of the Internet (perhaps our single most encompassing "web of inclusion"), she created a networked movement to fight violence against women called The International Network for the Rights of Female Victims of Violence in Pakistan. Its goals are twofold: (1) to bring the issue to public consciousness internationally and (2) to gather assistance for women who have been the victims of institutionalized and legally sanctioned violence called honor killings.

What's more, because Riffat has been involved with many efforts at interreligious dialogue over the years, she is aware that she has dug deeply enough into the root system that she is touching an issue which spans faith traditions: human rights. As a radical traditionalist, she chooses to resist religion in its own terms, and as a pluralist, she knows that she is doing so on behalf of all peoples.

> I believe very strongly that a paradigm for human liberation, for women's liberation, can be constructed within the framework of our religions, that our religions contain so many affirmations of human rights that we don't necessarily need to reject the religious framework in order to speak about human rights. So, in a way I am working within the tradition.

In her view, a purely secular campaign for human rights would not be as persuasive, especially to those with a faith-based worldview.

> If I want to reach the average Muslim woman — poor, illiterate, and rural — living in a village anywhere from Turkey to Indonesia, how do I do that? Can I go and say, "I bring you liberation in the name of the Universal Declaration of Human Rights, 1948?" Even if I could explain it to her, I don't think it would matter very much to her because it's totally outside her frame of reference. But if I say to her, "If you believe in God, and you believe that

God is just and merciful and compassionate, then do you think it is the will of this God that you should be beaten and brutalized and should die in childbirth?"

Riffat understands that simply posing this question once to any given Muslim will not be enough. Shifts in religious thinking take decades, even centuries to unfold. But they do occur. Bearers of religion are those who help bring focus and movement to the dialogue. Through her savvy use of the Internet, Riffat is turning up the heat on an issue whose time for transformation may be near. "I feel like it's an answer to such a serious and chronic problem. Once the dialogue is opened and becomes a subject of public debate, you can't kill it. But it involves, I think, a long-term effort to educate people — educate them in a spiritual sense, so that people begin to care about all human suffering and want to do something about it."

Embedded in the task of making better religious arguments is the need to find effective language with which to convey them. As we will see in the next chapter, this requires special sensitivity to context. It turns out that the women I spoke with are becoming multilingual in a new sense, experimenting with whether, where, and how to use religious language.

Chapter 6

FINDING THE WORDS
TO THEIR SONGS

Scanning stations on the car radio, we make quick intuitive choices about what we want to hear — rapper, reporter, evangelist, pop vocalist, talk show host. When we want company in the car, whose do we seek, and why? At the deepest level, what are such choices about? I think what Annie Dillard has noted about the written word holds true for spoken ones as well: "Why are we reading [and listening], if not in hope of beauty laid bare, life heightened and its deepest mystery probed? Why are we reading [and listening], if not in hope that the writer [or speaker] will magnify and dramatize our days, will illuminate and inspire us with wisdom, courage, and the hope of meaningfulness, and press upon our minds the deepest mysteries, so that we may feel again their majesty and power?"[30]

"If you name a thing, it *becomes*," the Navaho say. Words create realities. They become flesh — incarnations of thought and feeling. Well-named visions of reality are potentially the food of greater consciousness. If we are what we eat, it matters what naming we put on our plates.

Even though I am a minister, I tend to move the radio dial most quickly past evangelists whose language and manner seem intrusive, grating, and imperialistic. Yet a colleague of mine with a researcher's curiosity regularly tunes in to such programs to examine them from a sociological perspective. She considers them part of the picture of who we are. As a liberal, she knows that our future depends on deeper

123

engagement with those to the right of center on the theological and political spectrum. Even as we progressives are learning to recognize and express our kinship with our counterparts in other faith traditions — reform Jews and moderate Muslims, Hindus, and Buddhists for example — the greater challenge may be to reach across the divide to connect with those called orthodox and conservative. Beyond this is the ultimate challenge of creating some form of dialogue with the fundamentalist element in all of our traditions which seeks to claim an exclusive hold on truth. How can we talk to each other, as well as to secular humanists, about our most deeply held values in ways that honor our differences and cultivate all possible common ground?

Daring to Voice a Dream

On August 28, 1963, Martin Luther King Jr. expressed himself in a way that serves as a touchstone still. In the prophetic tradition, King held up a mirror to allow his listeners to pause, look at themselves, and recognize their part in the brokenness he named: America's default on promises made to all of its citizens. But King offered more than a mirror that day. He also held out a vision of a future which captured people's imaginations and inspired them to act in its behalf.

> I have a dream that one day this nation will rise up and live out the true meaning of its creed: "We hold these truths to be self-evident: that all men are created equal." I have a dream that one day on the red hills of Georgia the sons of former slaves and the sons of former slave owners will be able to sit down together at a table of brotherhood.
>
> When we let freedom ring, when we let it ring from every village and every hamlet, from every state and every city, we will be able to speed up that day when all of God's children, black men and white men, Jews and Gentiles, Protestants and Catholics, will be able to join hands and sing in the words of the old Negro

spiritual, "Free at last! free at last! thank God Almighty, we are free at last!"[31]

Keen to convey what he called "the fierce urgency of now," King called attention to the gap between the central vision of the American creed — *that all men are created equal* — and its yet imperfect realization. Serving as a physician to the collective soul, he diagnosed the condition of the moment and held out the hope that all could participate in the fulfillment of the dream. Without violating the separation of church and state, King describes progressive social values for an inclusive society in a tone ringing with spiritual valence. King the preacher remains true to his particular Christian context, yet chooses words which resonate with a broad spectrum of people, including secular humanists and Jews.

The "I Have a Dream" speech is a timeless prophetic message with political and social implications that extend far beyond the particular moment in history which prompted it. Many are inspired by it still, and hunger for contemporary leadership in the same prophetic vein. Yet forty years have passed since King delivered this speech, and in those years a very different segment of the religious spectrum has come to dominate the public airwaves. In fact, in the intervening years the Religious Right has been so savvy in using the media to broadcast its values that many Americans now have difficulty appreciating that a full spectrum of religious viewpoints still exists. In the public imagination, religion is at risk of simply being equated with the particular visions offered by conservatives, or even radical fundamentalists. Though some might consider this a victory of the highest order, others recognize the deprivation it represents and feel a responsibility to respond.

Completing the Picture

Helen Hunt reinforced this for me when she said: "To shy away from religious language gives all the religious language to the Right to shape and define very ancient terminology from one political perspective. Those of us in the progressive social movement have a real onus on us right now to use those terms and shape them in a way that matches our value system." Helen was quick to add that she does not envision this as a battle. "The Right is doing what it's doing for maybe some good reasons, but I think it's incomplete and that we do a real injustice to back off and let them just go forward. We need to complete the picture. We've got to get in there and expand their definitions of some of the terminology."

Linda Tarry-Chard, who has devoted much of her life to creating links across lines of diversity that usually divide us, also spoke strongly about the desirability of hearing a mix of voices on any given issue. Reflecting on the dominance of the Religious Right in the public sphere, she noted: "They do get visibility and there is a place for them at the table, but there are a host of other denominations, even within the most conservative denominations, that are someplace else on the spectrum, and they too have an influence on society." Like Helen, she feels a sense of urgency about creating more places at the table and, ironically, feels indebted to the Religious Right for creating the kind of momentum that may bring that into being.

> The visibility of the Religious Right is not necessarily bad. A lot of what they espouse gets people thinking. All of a sudden you're thinking about prayer and the possibility of your children praying in school. Now you may disagree with that, but it still means that dinnertime conversation gets to be about how you're going to respond. So you're talking about prayer, as opposed to talking about something else. If I may use the analogy, it functions almost like a correction in the stock market. These more visible or vocal conservative elements — whether in Judaism or Christianity or Islam — are forcing us into action.

The goal, then, is not to drown out conservative voices, but rather for progressives and moderates from all religious traditions to become vocal partners in a broader, more robust public conversation about what matters most. As Riffat Hassan told us in the last chapter, it is a question of learning to make better religious arguments, especially in public settings.

What does this entail? I questioned each of the women leaders closely on her use of religious language and imagery. Nearly all of them understand their leadership and work through a spiritual lens. That is, what they believe about God and God's requirements for faithful living informs what they do. But do they explicitly convey this to the people around them? If so, when? If not, why not? Does their language change if the audience shifts from individuals to congregations, from politicians to the public at large?

I discovered that these women are highly sensitive to both the risks and potential of using explicitly religious language, or "God-talk" as I call it. They use it, but they do so consciously and selectively. Their overriding concern is to be inclusive and effective. They are actively experimenting with religiously valenced language that reaches a broad audience yet still conveys the essential and distinctive values of their traditions. Listening to them explain how they are doing this sheds a new light on the silence of the Left in recent decades. It is not so much that they have been passively ceding to the Right during this time, it is that they have been actively wrestling with the need to find new words to their songs — words that effectively name the movement of Spirit in public settings which are both religiously diverse and significantly secular. They have undergone a kind of necessary muteness while being pressed to develop a greater degree of consciousness about faith itself and the myriad forms it may take. Now they are emerging from this period of muteness bearing the gifts of the wrestling: consciousness itself — about the power of language, about who is listening and with what receptors, about what can no longer be assumed of an audience, about the symbols and values which are central to their own and other faith traditions.

Consciousness of Context

When I asked Ginny Thornburgh if she used religious language when lobbying on Capitol Hill for disability issues, she immediately laid out this more nuanced stance toward context.

> I use faith language carefully. I assess the person. I'm not ashamed to be known as a woman of faith. But I also am smart and I usually have an agenda, and the point is, how are you going to get across what you want to say? It depends on the person. So I use language carefully.

She finds that naming things differently has been key to her work in the disability field and says that the emphasis on language in the multicultural community and the women's movement has been a helpful prod. "I just think it keeps us sharp and keeps us conscious." She has learned not to make assumptions about her audience, but instead to make space for them to tell her how they feel about matters of faith.

> For example, if I'm newly meeting someone, I'll ask, "Is faith important to you?" That's a wonderful way. It's like not assuming that people have children. Instead you say to people, "Tell me about your family." Then they'll either tell you about mother and father and aunts and uncles, or they'll tell you about whatever. So there are ways to get information.

Linda Tarry-Chard concurred. "Using religious language depends on the audience and the circumstance. You have to be able to meet people where they are and not project where you think they ought to be. Your message might be a very good one, but they won't hear it. Yet that same person, at a different time and place in their life and your life, maybe because of a relationship you have built, might be able to hear that same language." When I asked her how she had developed this sensitivity, she said:

> Trial and error. I put my foot in my mouth enough times and got a negative response. Also just gaining maturity and experience. My grandmother used to say, "Watch and pray." Well, you can't do a lot of watching and praying while you're talking. But if you're quiet, I find you can be more observant. You'll see the subtle little things, the body language of another person, the facial expression, and you'll know if you're on the right track or if you're really off.

As Linda reminded me, all of the information is right there in front of you. It is a matter of devoting time to being actively receptive to the other. Especially revealing is the way the person across from you is using language. "If you listen to what they say and how they say it, you can learn a lot about people, if you take that time and if you're willing to give that much of yourself — which, given how we live our lives, myself included, we're not often willing to do because we've got too much to do."

This investment of care and consciousness is necessary even within contexts which are more explicitly religious. For instance, Barbara Dobkin, founder of Ma'yan, the Jewish Women's Project, told me of the challenges of trying to sponsor change throughout the entire Jewish community. This involves honoring the stances of the entire spectrum of denominations from Orthodox to Reform, as well as cultural Jews who are non-observing. Simultaneously, she is experimenting with integrating feminist insights with Judaism: "It's looking at text in a new way, in an acceptable way. It's beyond angry. It's rethinking what it means to be a Jewish woman." As she juggles all of these considerations, she is also trying to avoid being typecast.

How can you talk about religion without sounding — I don't want to say, like a fanatic — but I think there is some way we have come to look at people of faith askew, and whether it's that we think of fundamentalists, or the radical right of any religion, I don't know. But there's something there.

Barbara framed the complexity well, acknowledging that if one does speak of faith in public, there is an immediate need to create in the public's mind an awareness of religious spectrum, to make it clear that one is offering a view that differs from the prevailing message of the Religious Right. One must also grapple with the reality that we lack a widely shared language that people from different backgrounds can use in speaking about their faith. This is compounded when multiple faith traditions are taken into account. "Sin" and "forgiveness" might have similar meanings among Christian groups, but very different meanings for Jews and Muslims, and different still for secularists. "Faith" is not a word that translates easily for some Jews, and there are Jews who consider themselves observant who do not believe in God. Likewise, many Buddhists do not believe in a supreme being, while Hindus find the notion of one God far too narrow and confining.

Some of the women told me they had deliberately chosen to downplay explicit discussions of faith because that had seemed the best way to honor the diversity around them. Reflecting on this, Laura Jervis admitted: "Maybe I was being a little too self-aware, but I didn't want WSFSH to be identified as a Christian organization, particularly because of the Jewish community we live in, and wanting that to be valued. And now we have a lot of people who are Muslim who work for WSFSH."

Ganga Stone, founder of God's Love We Deliver, was also concerned about inclusiveness:

I never used God-talk because I wanted to enroll as many different kinds of people — especially those who never use the G-word and didn't have any connection there — in doing what Mother Teresa charmingly described as "something beautiful for God." Clearly it's for God. That's a given. It's on the paychecks, it's on the invoices, it's on every single thing we do, so that's understood. But the meal is the message. No God-talk.

Clearly her own motives were faith-based, but she chose to convey that "under the radar" to both employees and clients. When I pressed her to say why, she again referred to inclusiveness, as well as the desire to protect vulnerable clients from possible abuses of their freedom.

> I wanted to have an environment in which everyone would be equally at home, and so if I have gay atheists, and I'm coming at them with some God-talk, how can that be fair? It's an invasion. If someone came in and wanted to volunteer so they could get access to our clients and do God-talk, I sent them to work in the kitchen washing dishes. If someone's sick and dying and they don't have receptors for God-talk, how dare you take advantage of their vulnerability and need for the food to come at them with your notion of wisdom.... There's only one answer to hunger: it's food.

Like Ganga, Lee Hancock knows that religious language can create pain for some people, particularly those who feel rejected and judged by traditional religious institutions or people. Yet rather than refraining from using it altogether, she has found that she can effectively use a substitute to suggest some of the same issues: "I work in environments where religious language is a source of great pain. I would not use religious language in the HIV/AIDS community. But I will use the spirituality language of the twelve-step program, since some people are familiar with that."

Lee considers this sensitivity to context a natural part of her job: "As a pastor I always mirror other people's language. And if you're also serving as a bridge, trying to build relationships between people, it becomes sort of multiple. Then you have to speak in tongues, in a way, because you're trying to hear the system of language that each person uses."

Beyond Mirroring

The question is, can one do more than mirroring? Are progressive religious leaders willing to risk using explicitly religious language in public settings where it might not be expected but could still have strategic power? It seemed to me that several of the women were feeling more comfortable with doing so, even if earlier in their careers they had not been. Laura Jervis, for instance, wondered if a certain forthrightness gets diminished by all this attention to context.

> I do adapt to my audience — less now than I used to, but I do. I don't know how intentional this is, but I do think I give people only what I think they can take and move with a little bit. And I feel a little ambivalent about that sometimes. On the positive side, it could be interpreted that I'm really connected to my audience and I know what they can receive and maybe how to carry them a little bit in a different direction. And the negative is that maybe I'm being a little disingenuous, that I'm not consistent in my articulation of a vision. So it's a little bit of a conflict for me.

This conflict, and the desire to better express a vision, has prompted her to experiment further with words. She says she is coming into a new understanding of her Christian faith, one which sees it as part of a wider, more "universal" community of faith. She has come to feel that in order to honor its centrality in her life, she needs to speak of it rather than keep it compartmentalized. But because she also values inclusiveness, she has found ways to name it which honor the truths of other traditions. As she puts it, this involves invoking a faith understanding which is, in a sense, "beyond Christianity."

[This arises from my] own sense of comfort with the language and my own understanding and goal for an integrated life. . . . So I don't censor my language anymore, but I use terms like *transformation, redemption, incarnation,* those sorts of words, which I believe are not just the product of Christianity, but of a really more universal kind of language. Certainly, my initial understanding is Christian, but these words are greater — beyond Christianity.

It is not that she has abandoned Christianity, but rather that she now senses how its core teachings are perhaps fed by deep impulses which flow into other faith traditions as well. When she now speaks of faith, she tries to conjure up those places of resonance.

Mychal Springer, in charge of chaplaincy training at Beth Israel Hospital when I interviewed her, was also becoming bolder about certain kinds of religious language, in part because of the influence of fundamentalist staff members who did not hesitate to voice their own understandings of faith.

What they've taught me is that if I can speak a more solidly religious language, then the hidden religiosity in many people will be nourished. . . . Because I'm a rabbi and it's a Jewish hospital, you've got to be respectful that people may or may not be believers. Jews never push, or at least liberal Jews never push a particular religious faith on anybody, so I don't feel like I'm in danger of that. But if I risk putting in the more mysterious aspects, I always receive the feedback that people are with me.

Those "more mysterious aspects," especially in a hospital setting, have to do with accompanying people as they ponder the wonder of birth or the transition toward death, the purpose of human existence, why hardship strikes some more than others, or the reality of seemingly miraculous healing. Mychal was finding that staff and patients alike welcomed such conversations.

Speaking Out: Some Specific Strategies

Like Mychal and Laura, other women were discovering effective ways to express the insights of a progressive faith. They outlined several strategies.

Story-Telling with Ordinary Language

Some communicate with a broad audience by selectively relinquishing traditional religious vocabulary and shifting into the vernacular. Gretchen Buchenholz, who prefers not to be considered a religious leader, feels that the stories of impoverished children carry a powerful ethical message just as they are. "Children," she insists, "will tell you very clearly what is right and what is wrong." She told me of the ten-year-old who said that every day when he goes to school he puts his head down on his desk because it hurts to be hungry. He is certain that when's he is president, no child will go hungry — a declaration of public responsibility that translates across cultures, religions, and boundaries of all kinds.

Sister Helen Prejean is a master story-teller. She relies on "very ordinary, accessible language" with occasional context-sensitive references to Biblical imagery. Her goal is to humanize people on Death Row, so she tells audiences as truthfully as possible of her own experiences with them. She feels that we evolve morally as we become more connected with one another. "In story-telling," she told me, "you can bring a person really close to a situation and help them to identify with the people in the story, and that's the key thing. Because what makes the death penalty possible — or any violation of human rights — is a mentality that some people are not human the way the rest of us are, and so anything we do to them is permissible." She does quote Scripture passages, like those which offer comfort to those who are suffering, such as "the last shall be first." Mostly, she appeals to common human experience.

> I emphasize with them what people of goodwill — regardless of their religious belief — can deal with. For example, stressing human rights, that no one should be tortured, no one should be killed. I'm going to talk about the mental anguish, the nightmares everyone has on Death Row: "they're coming to get me, and then I wake up and I'm sweating, realizing, no it's not time." I make it all incarnate through the stories of people they can identify with.

Using Words That Straddle

Other women are working to reframe traditional religious or theological terms so that they may be more broadly understood. As we have seen, Laura Jervis is doing this by using words like "transformation." It is almost like building a new lexicon. Helen Hunt, for instance, offered this possible amplification of the word "spirituality."

> John Trudell is a Native American who says spirituality is responsibility, and when we're responsible for our neighbor, responsible for our context, that's a spiritual perspective. So you don't sleep at night thinking that the world is fine while anyone is in poverty or anyone is hungry, because you are responsible for them. Spirituality is love in action.

Borrowing from Native American perspectives, Helen is crafting a new language of meaning which straddles the sacred and the secular. She is particularly interested in finding language that fosters a conversation between secular feminists and religious feminists, two groups whose strengths might be leveraged together were it not for language barriers.

When I began to talk about spiritual empowerment, some of the feminists I've worked with didn't understand what I meant. They said the women's movement is secular, and I said, you may think it's secular, but I think the women's movement is about liberating the human spirit, and that to me is spiritual work, not secular work.

Lee Hancock prefers words that have meaning both in and outside of religious contexts. "It's one of the reasons I like activism in the public square," she told me. "Prophetic language has more of a bridging quality — the language of social issues. You know, we can talk about peace, justice, and reconciliation. Justice is a word that straddles. My dissertation is about suffering. That's another word that straddles. And, increasingly, so is healing."

Part of Helen Prejean's method is to provide translations between ordinary and religious language as she is telling her stories. In the same breath, she refers to "getting in touch with your deepest desires" and "aligning ourselves with the energy of God." Ginny Thornburgh told me she is part translator and part teacher, even when speaking to religious groups.

I'll say, "In your church, parish, synagogue, temple, mosque, or meeting house," because I want them to see that these principles of welcome and hospitality apply across the board. And so I'll use *congregation* mostly, but then I'll remind them. And I've learned that even while in most groups you can say *church* and *synagogue*, every once in a while our Catholic friends and our Episcopal friends like to hear the word "parish."

Using Moral Language as a Stand-In

Helping people discern right and wrong, and especially the gray areas in between, is the role of the public religious leader. The women I interviewed often had to call politicians and the public-at-large to account on social issues that affect the common good. Yet "speaking truth to power" entails certain risks. One must be prepared to stand out and create conflict. There is the possibility of being ignored, dismissed, talked down, fired, or even assassinated.

Here is where being rooted in one's convictions, coupled with the knowledge that one is part of a community of others who hold similar views, provides the necessary ballast. The goal in such speech is to offer a different set of criteria for the choice at hand, to activate the conscience and compassion of those in power in a way that allows them to save face and act on behalf of a larger purpose.

Laura Jervis told me of times when she needs to speak her truth to city officials. Recognizing that ministers do still carry a certain moral authority in people's minds, she deliberately invokes that. Yet she still chooses her language carefully. She told me of an instance where a commissioner of Homeless Services had proposed setting quotas and incentives for social workers based on the number of homeless people they placed in independent housing. She felt the underlying logic of the policy violated the religious teaching that all lives are of equal worth in the eyes of God. Yet she challenged him with language that had a clear moral valence but did not explicitly refer to God.

> It was really one of those toe-to-toe conversations about the value of one person's life over another. I questioned him about putting a bounty on people's lives. What if it took one social worker two years to build the trust of an individual resident, whereas another person came in and in three months they were able to move on with their lives? It was really kind of laying on the moral piece with him.

Gretchen Buchenholz, who prefers a generic moral language to explicitly religious language, regularly uses it in speeches and in conversation with the press. Again, it takes the form of offering a different yardstick. In a suit against the state of New Jersey opposing the ware-housing of babies, she challenged the culture's definition of success: "you don't measure civilized society by its gross national product, but by how many infants make it through the first year." If she had been using religious language, she might have spoken of God's preference for the "least of these." Both convey an ethic of accountability toward the impoverished and disenfranchised.

Alisa Del Tufo told me she works similarly, boldly using words like *sin* and *evil* when speaking in public about issues of domestic violence. "I use it in policy conversations. I use it in talks I give to groups. I use it in writing. And I use *compassion* a lot."

Developing a Multilingual Capacity

Scholar Walter Brueggemann has noted that "people of faith in public life must be *bilingual*. They must have a *public language* for negotiation at the wall. And they must have a more *communal language* for processing behind the gate, in that community."[32] His metaphor is helpful but incomplete for understanding the language skills these women are developing. For him, "negotiation at the wall" means in the market-place or public arena; "behind the gate" means within the community of a particular faith tradition. But with their heightened attention to context and their growing ability to match language to it, these women are actually moving beyond bilingual to multilingual.

Speaking in a variety of tongues is a competency that progressive religious leaders must develop to communicate effectively in an increasingly diverse culture. Certainly those who hope to lead still need to be formed and supported by specific language and ritual within a particular tradition, as well as be persuasive with the secular language of the public arena. But now there is a need for fluency of a third kind — one which can give voice to a universal language of meaning appropriate for a complex milieu that is at once multicultural, religiously plural, and significantly secular. Increasingly, the task for a progressive religious leader is to be able to interpret, translate, and teach across a variety of domains so as to raise awareness of deeper truths that bind us together all across the spectrum. It is to continually view citizenship through the eyes of faith, while speaking of it in the vernacular of the current context, and periodically offering links to entirely different subcultures.

Jan Orr-Harter's way of working on nuclear disarmament with various groups is an example of the bilingual mode. With church groups, she used "language from behind the wall," suggesting, for example, that liberation from the power of the military industrial complex was a form of the ancient story of Exodus. But with a political person "at the gate" her language changed: "With a political person, you have to be political, and you have to translate the numbers of people, the groups, the endorsements." At this point she was carefully using biblical imagery in one context and purely political arguments in another. But as Lee Hancock suggests, it may be even more fruitful and provocative to swap language back and forth across realms.

> I assume, because I live in a secular world, that religious language for the most part is not understood, and that it may alienate or create hostility. I would never use a language of orthodoxy. By that I mean I wouldn't talk about omnipotence. Instead I would talk about power. I would make those kinds of translations. And although I'm not gifted in this way, I think there's some virtue in moving back and forth between sacred and secular — like if you're using secular concepts, try linking them with biblical illustrations. I certainly use religious language in the classroom, but in terms of any other place — I mean, I'm married to a secular Jew. The discourse in my family can be highly charged spiritually but it's not insider religious language.

"Insider" language, then, while it still functions as an essential touchstone, can easily create barriers and function to exclude others. If our overarching ethic is finally one of inclusiveness and relationship, we need to be vigilant about voicing the translations and analogies that will help us to understand one another.

Connie Baugh repeatedly traversed the sacred-secular divide in her work as minister of the Church of Gethsemane and director of the associated multifaith non-profit, JusticeWorks. She noted that she is most fully herself when speaking openly in her native tongue — that is, in the language of faith. "I can take a good sermon and convert it to secular speech," she told me, "but I'm much more connected when I am using the language of my faith and the language of my religious convictions. It's just much more who I am. I can do both, but it's not my preference."

Still, because of her passion to express her religious convictions to the broadest possible audience, she has become fluent in other modes and was able to give me a number of examples:

> In a religious community, you could talk about every human being is a child of God. In the secular community, you had to talk about every human being has value, and no one is expendable. And, although most people in the secular world recognized that the passion with which I spoke was religiously motivated, I never spoke with terms that weren't acceptable. So, empowerment, advocacy, legislative change, progressive left, the common good — all those I used.
>
> I liked talking about public life. I could often use what I feel about humanity and the poorest of the poor by simply not talking about each person being in the image of God, but talking about the common bonding... that in public life, the more we recognize our connectedness, the better our public life would be. And in communion, I say *communion* means common union. We are first united under humanity, and then we're united in our faith.

For Connie, the discipline to offer these definitions arises from a single guiding principle: "Faith is the commitment to participate in life, with God, in the ongoing creation and liberation of the world. With progressives, I talk about that in terms of the struggle for justice being the commitment not to leave anyone behind." This is why she acts and speaks as she does. This is why it is worth it to her to make the extra effort to be understood.

Riffat Hassan's passion is to make better religious arguments within the conservative Islamic world. Though she too can make translations for secular contexts, her particular emphasis is on how best to counteract the logic of fundamentalists. She explained how clever maneuvering is necessary in openly patriarchal Muslim countries when approaching the subject of women's rights.

> I can't go to any country, any city or college and say I want to teach a course about women's rights in Islam, because immediately it would raise a lot of red flags and the conservatives would protest. But if I say I want to talk about Koranic ethics, I want to talk about the universal principles of Koranic teaching, like the right to justice, right to education, right to freedom, I think I could do it. That would not arouse the same kind of resistance. And then once I start talking about Koranic ethics, I make the point that according to the Koran every Muslim man and woman should be educated. Well, are not women human beings? Why should they not be educated? So, in that way you can come at the same issue from a very different entry point, and you can be much more effective. Then it's more difficult for them to knock you down.

These are just a few examples of how the women I spoke with are experimenting with a language of the common good that conveys progressive faith perspectives to a broad and diverse constituency. Integrating concepts like interdependence and social transformation with specifically religious notions of resurrection and redemption, they are offering analogies, stories, and images capable of stirring our deepest yearnings and highest aspirations.

Venturing beyond Relativism

Moving into this multilingual mode involves several large challenges. One is avoiding the value-free stance of pure relativism, where all views are seen as equally valid and none more deserving of our commitment than another. While this is usually a necessary step beyond feeling that one's own view of reality is the only one, we are not well served if it becomes a lasting conviction about how life is. We cannot act ethically — that is, with some sense of responsibility to uphold the sacredness and dignity of all of life — if we truly believe that it does not matter what we do. We function best amid the swirling complexity of competing viewpoints if we hold to some guiding star, if we achieve some perspective that gathers multiplicity into some larger vision of wholeness. There is a kind of coagulation of life experience that can carry a person to such a place, yet it still takes courage to take those first steps into it, and to find the words to describe what one sees there.

There are other risks. By moving from a language rooted in a specific religious tradition toward a language that "straddles," some of the power of particularity is lost. "Every human being is a child of God" offers a point of reference, a primary Source — namely God — that is very different from "every human being has value." References to God may motivate the person of faith, whereas the notion that "every human being has value" may or may not awaken the moral compass of more secular listeners.

One of the ways I try to get around the watered down impotence of generalities is to use religious language educationally. I try to open people's minds to the values that different faith traditions share as well as to their distinctions. In speaking of justice I might say: "In a Christian context or idiom, the pursuit of justice involves becoming Christ-bearers in the world, incarnating love, becoming the body of Christ in the world by working for justice and peace for all of God's children. The equivalent for Jews might be to follow the requirement to pursue *tikkun olam,* or the repair of the world which actually prompts Jews to become involved with people outside their own community. Speaking of financial giving or philanthropy, I might use stories from each tradition to illustrate the mandate to give freely from one's own resources. "God loves a cheerful giver in the New Testament is mirrored in the Koranic saying, "If you have two dates, you must share one." One of the most satisfying moments in the Face to Face youth program that I co-direct was when an Israeli Jewish girl quoted the Koranic teaching about the sharing of dates with a hungry person because she had been so moved by this vivid image of giving from another tradition.

Voicing faith perspectives in these ways places new demands on religious leaders, whether lay or clergy. It means that they must evidence both a particular worldview and special competencies. The worldview is suggested by the phrase that sometimes accompanies the reading from the Bible in a Protestant worship service, "There is still more light to be shed from the Word," meaning that truth is never fixed but in process, that what we believe and interpret about God's word to us in any moment is partial and limited, that God's truth surpasses human comprehension or expression. This stance, which stands in stark contrast to fundamentalism, involves a certain humility — the awareness that we are all fallible and may be wrong. It also means that wherever we stand religiously, however deeply committed, we are open to engaging with other traditions and learning from them in ways that may complement or correct our own.[33] For a religious leader to express this worldview implies multifaith competency or knowledge of other religious traditions and appreciation for them. Such competency

involves more than intellectual knowledge of the basics of world religions and includes being moved by their teachings and seeing them
as living, changing entities shaped by communities of belief through
ritual, liturgy, and action.

Another challenge to crafting a public language of meaning is evident if we look back at the Martin Luther King Jr. speech from the
beginning of the chapter. The words themselves have a poetry about
them that would move most people, yet they are particularly potent for
those who understand the historical context. "We hold these truths"
has deeper resonance for listeners who know that they come from the
Declaration of Independence, and who know the rest of the words
to the spiritual, "Free at Last, thank God Almighty I'm free at last."
Because most Americans (even church-going ones) are biblically illiter-
ate and because we are ever more religiously diverse, a speaker can no
longer assume that everyone shares texts or understands the particular
references. The groom we met in chapter 5 is the perfect example of
someone who resonated with the breaking of the glass in a Jewish wedding but knew nothing about the history of the ritual or its meaning
within the tradition. This means that the most powerful of speakers
will be those who find ways to bring back into public awareness those
deep guiding images that spring from the root system of our faith
traditions. We can no longer simply repeat the same old formulas. We
must dive deeper and take nothing for granted.

Such challenges should not deter us from the goal of claiming public
space for a broader range of voices to express the pluralism that we
say we value. Progressive religionists need to add our visions of the
future to the more conservative ones that are already in full view there.
Not to do so cedes this influential public territory not only to the
Religious Right, but also to secular humanists who believe that faith
has no place in shaping public debate or our moral fabric. We see
the advanced forms of this in secularized European countries which
attempt to sanitize the public square from religious influences.

I believe that progressive religionists need to do what these women leaders are doing — experimenting with a language of meaning that translates broadly. Yes, there is the risk of alienating people. Yes, there will be charges (misguided ones, I believe) that the separation of church and state is being violated. But yes, a greater and more complete story will thus be told. Maya Angelou has written, "There is no agony like bearing an untold story inside of you."[34] If progressives remain silent, we relinquish our proper role in a great shift toward a more adequate embrace of our wholeness. The "fierce urgency of now" is that unless we speak, we may lose the ability to convey our deepest convictions and hopes for our common life together. Finding this distinctive public voice will forge a new identity for progressives as culture shapers and consensus builders, defusing the now dangerous escalation of fundamentalist energies.

Chapter 7

LIVING A
SEAMLESS LIFE

In earlier chapters, we have seen that the holding environments these leaders created function primarily as vessels of resistance, offering critiques and correctives to unjust or neglectful mainstream structures and systems. We have seen women practicing alternative modes of leadership and actively experimenting with new ways to bring a moral perspective to bear on public issues. These too may be understood as acts of resistance — against the norm of invisibility for public religious leadership and the constraints of traditional definitions. Taken together, all of these activities reveal a substantial investment of energy and a remarkable capacity for taking risks and living creatively at the margins of mainstream culture, often with minimal recognition and support. Many might consider such work extraordinarily difficult, sometimes dangerous, and often thankless.

In light of this, it is important to note that nearly all of these women are veterans within their chosen spheres, having been engaged in their work for over a decade and most for upward of twenty years. Only three left their organizations either for an extended sabbatical or to pursue something else, like child-rearing. Clearly, these leaders have staying power — the ability to sustain a public presence over the long haul, often midwifing organizations, causes, and clients through many cycles of change and growth. They are loyalists to causes, not simply well-intentioned dabblers in public service. Countering the current trend toward pursuing several careers over the course of a lifetime, transferring one's "skill set" from one arena to another, these women have made enduring commitments of self and soul.

How are they able to do this? What does it take to give oneself wholeheartedly to those who are in great need or to continually immerse oneself in the evidence of structural injustice? Do these women feel burdened by what they do or experience a sense of sacrifice? Can they really claim to have any balance in their lives — that elusive goal touted by every self-help book on the shelf? In short, what is the secret of sustaining a resistance faith?

As we shall see in this chapter, the answer is paradoxical: sustaining resistance is both costly and deeply energizing. Principally, it involves a capacity to see and respond to injustice and evil without being consumed by it. This takes a certain toll, but also confers a deep sense of being involved in meaningful action on behalf of Life. What these women told me was that these forces play against each other within what feels like a seamless whole — a definition of balance that self-help books rarely touch upon. In this area, as in so many others, these women leaders are holding to a different ethic than that of the collective. For them, achieving balance is not some plate-spinning trick for "having it all." Instead, they actually live as if "having it all" means "having justice for all" — an ever-renewing motivation to fill the gap between what is and what could be.

Counting the Costs

In the many hours I spent talking with these women, terms like burnout or fatigue rarely came up. Instead, there was a prevailing sense of energy and vitality. Yet when I specifically asked about the costs of the work, many did name some, citing a few as significant and others as just part of the territory.

The Usual Suspects

When you combine entrepreneurial with non-profit, certain stresses are inevitable. Foremost is the need for hard work. As Joan Campbell, former General Secretary of the National Council of Churches, explained, this is the non-glamorous side of leadership: "I think one of the things that often gets missed when people define leaders as visionary and charismatic is that you really work twenty-four hours a day, and you do put your life on hold. I'm quite sure that if I had a husband and young children to raise that I couldn't do what I do now." But in the same breath, she affirmed that this investment feels worth it to her: "Other people might think of it as a sacrifice, but I don't. I've chosen this task. To the degree that I can be responsible for making some things happen that I think are important and change life for people, then I can sleep very well."

For Ruth Messinger and others, the loss of family time is a source of tension, but one which seems worth bearing. In answer to my question about sacrifices, Ruth said: "I don't think it's a cost or a sacrifice. It's the way in which I live my life, the way I believe life should be lived. Has it occasionally put me at odds with my family? Yes, because I do it in a fairly consuming way. But it's what I wanted to do. I'm happier doing it than not doing it."

The women also mentioned financial stresses, but even notoriously low non-profit salaries did not seem to be foremost on their minds. Instead it was the constant pressure to secure funding. As Alisa Del Tufo explained, this is a double drain on the real work of the organization.

> We may be getting some more public money in the future, but for the most part it's been private, which is an ongoing burden. I've been raising money for pretty much twenty years, and it's a tiring and difficult part of what I do. We have always had just enough money to do what we need to do but it's a constant battle getting it. Wishful thinking is that there would be some more stability in

our funding sources so that there isn't so much effort going into just raising money, and so that we could spend more time and energy doing real work.

In a larger sense, attracting funding is about the ongoing challenge of convincing others of the value of the work. Laura Jervis spoke of this as a question of generating public will. As she explained, in our current political climate, more and more effort must go into creating the notion that it is actually in our best interests to be responsible for one another.

> The biggest obstacle is the lack of Government will, public will. And compassion fatigue. There is, I think, this sense of individualism that has crept back into our society, or maybe it was always there. . . . It's the whole conservative movement. The notion that people should be able to do this themselves, that a single mother with three children should be able to get to her WEP assignment to sweep floors every day at 8:00, no matter what. There's such a diminishing sense of community — that we're all in this together and we need to help each other. So holding up that value and that voice is an effort.

As we shall see, valuing something which the collective does not, or to which it pays mere lip service, can be deeply draining. For those who practice a resistance faith, there may be little or no reassuring mirroring from the society at large — no day-to-day messages which communicate "we see you and support your efforts." There is a daily need to stand against the tide, to counter the considerable force of the status quo. To survive over the long haul, these women have not only cultivated steady, grounded convictions about more just, humane ways to live, they have developed strategies for continually feeding and renewing these convictions. Jan Orr-Harter, for instance, talked about her ability to persevere as a combination of ego strength and vision:

"You need to be willing to take all the scars that are going to come your way, to develop that ego hide. . . . Part of what vision does for the leader is that it helps you survive all the little things that could throw you off course. . . . You have to develop a pretty strong hide and a sense of who you are and not be constantly blown by the winds. This doesn't mean you're rigid or inflexible . . . just that you will continue to exist beyond the present crisis."

Lee Hancock identified another potentially costly dynamic specific to the grassroots approach which many of these women leaders employ. "I find myself starting over a lot," she told me. "Though each time I'm wiser than before, it still takes lots of cardinal energy [initiating energy] to create something anew. It always takes a toll on my health, which is ironic [since health is my primary focus]. Grassroots work is about starting at the bottom. You're always the new kid on the block, interpreting the work to people. It's not usually about building and maturing, working from a base that already has resources and a reputation." Again the absence of resources and reputation. As with the funding issue, there is this sense of having nothing to lean on, of having to introduce and prove oneself afresh in setting after setting.

Finally, there is the sheer publicness of leadership to contend with — the pressure to be on, present, and responsive wherever one goes. As Laura Jervis noted, "It's rare to walk out the front door and not know someone or not hear about a problem, or to be asked to get involved with a particular issue or to find someone housing. So there is this feeling of never being off, never being able to retreat." While acknowledging the reality of this dynamic, Laura and others accommodated it into a larger view of the nature of the work. In so doing, Sr. Helen Prejean even took issue with the word "cost."

Working against any kind of injustice is what many people call an uphill battle. It requires what I call "expenditure" rather than sacrifice. You have to work at it. But in your imagination you don't perceive it as this uphill thing. Your vision is that we're on this road, we're all going to wake up eventually, and we're trying to help us wake up sooner, believing in peoples' goodness and decency. If you want to focus on just the expenditure part of it, then yes, it's not easy to get on planes and be among a lot of strangers all the time. It's much easier to be home, water my flowers, and be able to write. But I start getting restless when I'm home too long, like I know that God just put me here and this is what I've got to do. So yes, there's expenditure, but what you focus on is the love and passion that holds you to it.

Loss of Innocence: Looking Evil in the Eye

Consider the quality of love and passion that must be flowing through a woman to hold her to the task of accompanying someone to the execution chamber. Consider how it feels day in and day out to have one's clients be the abused and neglected of society: battered women, ex-prisoners, starving children, people dying of AIDS, the homeless, people no one else will touch. After her first experience on death row, in an act of what she called "pure self-preservation," Helen Prejean vowed to herself, "I'm never going back. It's just so horrendous." Annie Bovian, executive director of Women's Advocate Ministry, a program which advocates for much stronger rehabilitation programs in the criminal justice system, also saw something horrendous early in her career. During a field education placement in seminary, she was serving as a pastor in a city hospital when a young black prison inmate was admitted to have her baby. A heavy heroin user, imprisoned on drug charges, she had nevertheless stayed clean throughout her pregnancy, determined to mother a healthy child. The healing power of the relationship with the child caught Annie's attention. That's why she was all the more jolted by what happened next.

She had the most darling little boy. Oh, the baby looked as if he could pose for Gerber's, that's how beautiful and healthy this baby was. And then I was there on the day that she was getting ready to be taken back to prison. Her baby had to be taken from her because they didn't have a nursery, no program for mothers to spend time with their children. Her mother came, along with her sister, in order to take the baby. There were two correction officers standing there, giving her one last encounter with the baby. She had the baby in her arms, kissed him, and then turned him over to her mother. And almost with the speed of light the correction officers had shackles on her wrists and on her ankles. Now, other than in the movies, this was the first time I had ever seen anyone be shackled, and it was one of the most horrific experiences I've ever had. It brought back all sorts of images in my mind of slavery, the whole nine yards. And it happened so fast I screamed, the mother screamed, the baby almost dropped. She went down the elevator in shackles and the grandmother stood there with the baby in her arms. I mean, it just blew me away, it just blew me away. And even now I can see it just as clear in my mind. I think I'll keep that image for the rest of my life.

Though both women's clients were criminals by society's standards, it was not being in their presence that the women found horrendous — not being around their broken spirits, haunted eyes, street person smells, frightening logic, or faltering bodies. It was not, in short, the considerable otherness which the least of these can press upon us. Instead, it was witnessing what society does to them in the name of justice or out of our own disease and brokenness. To witness this open-heartedly is to experience an appalling lack of tenderness and responsibility for human life. It is to undergo a loss of innocence, a breakdown of the illusion that life is safe, predictable, and under control.

Like other women I interviewed, Helen and Annie felt an urge to turn away. They were not sure they could bear to see such things again. Helen admitted, "Your stomach is in knots. You're experiencing this terror that they're going to kill this guy. And when you're in the presence of families holding that kind of pain, their pain gets inside of you too." But both women followed a stronger urge — to bear witness to what they saw. Recall that one of Gretchen Buchenholz's first acts when she discovered children starving in New York was to make a phone call to the press. Helen and Annie each had that same instinct. Sr. Helen told me, "When I left the execution chamber that first time, I had a very clear sense of mission — that I needed to start sharing with people what I knew about the death penalty. I felt people would change once they heard the truth about it." Annie echoed this conviction that unconsciousness of injustice is what allows it to continue. Of the shackling incident, she said:

> It was horrible, and I think things like that the public needs to see. The public needs to see what it does to people who are incarcerated — males, females, even children. Now I understand that in New York...they're going to take them in at ten years old. My gosh, can't anybody save a ten-year-old kid? It's unbelievable. Boys and girls.

Here is where the analogies to the Holocaust come in, the questions about who knew what and when. After telling me such stories of things they had seen, several women wondered aloud if American society is slipping into similar territory, overlooking or rationalizing patterns which may rightfully be called evil. As Annie Bovian framed it:

> Racism has so permeated our society that most people can see it and not think there's anything wrong with it. There's a systemic problem with our criminal justice system and people do not want

to face it. I think that most whites feel very secure with the criminal justice system that we have today because, at least for now, their kids are not being picked up. But madness has no end, and the Germans found that out. The madness is forever permeating itself into one thing or another. When we get to a point now where we feel it's more important to build prisons than to build schools, that's evil. And I feel as if we need another Dietrich Bonhoeffer, or even a Martin Luther King Jr. — someone who's willing to see and name evil, like King did in his letter from the Birmingham jail.

Having the receptors and vision to look injustice, societal disease, and even evil in the eye and then work to bring them to public consciousness is the crux of what these women offer as bearers of a resistance faith. It is this dynamic which is at once dangerous, deeply wearying, and ultimately meaningful to them. One of the most wearying features of it is the embeddedness of the patterns which these leaders seek to change. Because of their own wiring, they initially cannot believe that the public, once alerted to the situation, will not readily take action to remedy it. But the reality is that there are all kinds of reasons why many people cannot or will not get on board. When entire social systems and long-practiced patterns of behavior need major overhaul, resistance, fear, and power struggles can run deep. Annie Bovian told me that after all of her years of building awareness, she is stunned and pained to discover that even people she considers allies do not always see what she sees.

It feels overwhelming to me when I speak with people who are supposed to have some sort of understanding in terms of what's going on out there, and I find they don't have a clue. Even some clergy people, or people who claim to be clergy-oriented. Or a member of the board telling me they prefer hearing what we do after the women get out of prison. And I say to myself, "My

Lord, what am I fighting here? What am I fighting here?" Because that's a dangerous level of ignorance.

Lee Hancock and Mychal Springer, both of whom are seeking to broaden concepts of healing, noted the tremendous resistance to change that underlies our current health care crisis. One of the burdens of the work is having the knowledge that, as a society, we may not muster the courage and will to reinvent ourselves. Lee confessed:

> I have this terrible apocalyptic vision every once in awhile. We're all sitting around bald-headed because everyone's undergoing chemo and no one's addressing the real causes of toxicity in our society. And there are no longer any parks because they're all landfills and that what's happened is that people go to doctors for totally outmoded methods of treatment. If you want to talk about the power of orthodoxy, the power of orthodoxy in medicine is so much more powerful than that of the church right now. People are terrified to be empowered on behalf of their own health, absolutely terrified.

As a chaplain in a major hospital, Mychal Springer was operating in the midst of this orthodoxy, trying to expand the notion of health to include attention to soul. The potentially wearying dynamic in such a situation is to be the one asking the questions that no one else is asking. For her, this even includes challenging underlying assumptions about how we think.

> I need to help people see that the Enlightenment idea that you can understand everything and fix everything falls short. The more miraculous are the things that Western medicine can do, the more control it appears to offer. But there's so much we still don't understand about how how it all holds together. Particularly with the elderly and newborns, we need better ways of addressing the complicated questions of who lives and when is it okay to

die. The more control we have, the more we need to proceed intentionally and with integrity. Along with all these procedures that help people live longer, we need to be asking, "Why?" If you haven't asked yourself what your life's about, what's the purpose of making it so long?

Focusing on such large, systemic issues entails two further threats to self. One is the possibility of being overwhelmed by the immensity of the task. As Jan Orr-Harter put it after years of slow work on nuclear disarmament issues, "It's a sacrifice to be willing to put yourself in a situation where you are going to feel inadequate, absorb some pain from that, and still have to function and go forward. There's an emotional toll." These women know they cannot do the work alone. Systemic issues are everyone's business, and the grassroots strategies that many of these women employ are designed to spread both consciousness and responsibility widely. But when people are in the grip of fear and resistance, they may not accept their share of the burden of transformation. When I asked Linda Tarry-Chard if there was anything she feared about leadership, she said it was the pressure to fix things that were not hers alone to fix.

We're making money god in our society right now, allowing great disparities between the haves and the have-nots, and our religiosity is going in directions that are not necessarily good for us as a society, so there's a great deal of confusion and fear. People look to leaders to make it all right, even when part of it is their own personal work to do, their own commitments to make. What happens is that if people feel you have some sort of spiritual center, they will look to you for more than maybe you can give. So that you become mother, confidante, big sister, financier — just all of it. And that's often more than what any one person can bear.

I Look at the World and Weep: Stories of Burnout

Sometimes it does become too much to bear. Connie Baugh, whose motivations are fiercely progressive, regularly lays herself open to societal pain. She is not afraid to name the threatening dynamics in our midst.

> I look at our world and weep. I weep because I think we are in such tremendous trouble. I think we're extremely sick, and the greatest symptom of that is the alienation we have from each other. You see that in the fact that we fear each other so greatly, and the greater the fear, the more privatized we become, and the more privatized, the less public life we have. The less public life we have, the more almost totalitarian we become. Why is that? Well, who challenges that political system? The public. But if there is no public, then you only have individuals, and no individual is going to be able to change a political system that's become as removed from the people as ours has in this country.

With the two organizations she spent twenty years building, Church of Gethsemane and Justice Works Community, she sought to engender at least a microcosm of healthy public life, where bridges between the disenfranchised and the elite promoted a more fully participatory democracy. But it was as if the illness she battled on the outside finally broke into her own body. Connie became critically ill with hepatitis C. She tried to continue working on a limited basis, but finally recognized that, at least for a time, she needed to "go into a cocoon." What convinced her was that not only was she drained of all physical stamina, she had lost hope. Still, it was a wrenching decision. "It was just so painful to think that I'd be leaving at a time when I probably could have had the most fun and simultaneously taken the church to the next level of growth. I felt like Moses when God said: 'Too bad, brother, you're not going to the Promised Land.' I never liked that story." Connie admits that having always defined herself in relation to justice issues, being in a place of not knowing what her body can handle and where she wants to plant herself, is deeply disconcerting.

> This is the first time in my life that I don't know where I'm going. Growing up, marching through college, the Vietnam war, the civil rights movement, the women's movement, and my own history merging with prison ministries — I just have always known what I was doing and how I wanted to do it. Now, having absolutely no idea is the scariest part. It's hard not to be right there on the line.

While several of the women I interviewed spoke of needing time for retreat and renewal, only two others reluctantly chose to leave the work for an extended period. For them, the cost to their families seemed too great. Ganga Stone, founder of God's Love We Deliver, noted the irony that though her work involved feeding a thousand people a day, both she and her daughter were beginning to starve on some deep spiritual and emotional level. "It just became so clear to me," she said, "that other people could do GLWD work at least as well as I could, if not better, and only one person could do what my daughter needed." Her own burnout, she felt, had occurred as her early one-on-one contact with clients was increasingly displaced by administrative duties, management, and fundraising. "I had no companionship, I had no spiritual conversation, I had no contemplation time, I had no time to be who I actually was. I was trapped in this role." Other women also cited this dynamic, but were able to adjust their responsibilities so that they retained the nourishment that one-on-one work with clients gave them.

Compensating Dynamics

I cannot help but wonder what kind of holding environments we might create that would offer succor to leaders like these. Further, what kinds of self-supporting strategies can leaders themselves use to counterbalance the wearying dynamics this work entails? We have seen that maintaining one-on-one contact with clients is not only energizing, it also provides ongoing insights into systemic issues. Measuring progress in small steps, and celebrating it, also helps sustain a sense of momentum, especially concerning those deeply embedded paradigm shifts which really can only unfold at glacial speed. When feelings of inadequacy arise, this perspective is crucial. As Jan Orr-Harter told me, it seems best to focus on what is doable and hold the long-term goals more loosely.

> You know it's always held together with band-aids and luck and love . . . so you just have to build it for today. Of course you're hoping to build something that will endure and be part of a long-term plan, but you can't get your heart wrapped up in building an empire, because empires have a way of falling apart.

Laura Jervis noted that there is a different sense of time that goes along with this perspective. "Producing and running buildings for the long haul has given me an odd perception of time. If it takes five years to build a project, that doesn't seem so bad to me. I don't get impatient." These women proceed modestly but with determination, knowing they are doing their appropriate part to move the glaciers along. As we saw in Gretchen Buchenholz' account in chapter 1, it is the sensation of being "a grain of sand building solutions" while belonging to "a transcendent something" — playing "the tiny role each of us plays in this unimaginably immense galaxy."

Several of these women told me that collegial connections with other women were key to their being able to sustain challenging work as public leaders. Linda Tarry-Chard first learned this as a child growing up in the Black church where she depended on older women as mentors and teachers. Though her support circle was at first confined to the African-American community, across the years she has developed an ever broader circle of women friends from diverse backgrounds.

Laura Jervis told me that challenges from her "cabal" of women friends are just as important as their support. This group makes her take risks she might not have on her own.

My little cabal of women friends is really very important to me. We intersect at these wonderful moments and points, and we talk about each other as lifelines. There's nothing we can't talk about, and that's great. . . . We have dinner together once a month for like four hours. They're a touchstone for me. It's just wonderful. . . . Not only are we compatible personally, although our lives are very different, but we think alike and have the same kinds of critiques about issues facing the city. And, we push each other. You know, if one of us — I think it's usually me — is being a little timid — there's that push to be more courageous. I don't know what I would do without it.

Other traditional restorative practices are important to remember — like taking time for Sabbath and rest, or simply allowing oneself to play. Contemplative practices drawn from the world's great religious traditions and those that restore connection to the body, like yoga or running, are especially helpful as a counterbalance to demands for constant action and response.

But the single most effective restorative dynamic in these leaders' lives was not a self-conscious strategy at all. It was the fact that the work itself gave back even more than it asked of them. At least half did not even consider their work to involve sacrifice.

Feeling on Fire

The more dominant emotion expressed by these leaders was their deep satisfaction, sense of purpose, and meaningful contribution to society. This enviable engagement with their work helped to sustain them, to survive setbacks and discouragement, and even to thrive. "Never bored" was how Lee Hancock put it.

> This guy [at a party] was asking me some questions, and then I was just on fire. And he said, "I'm so envious of you. I have a job; I get paid an enormous amount of money to do my job, but you are so alive. You make a difference." . . . Well, for starters, I'm never bored, and boredom is just my idea of being in hell. I mean, there are things that I do that are tedious, but I'm not bored, and I think that's a tremendous gift in this cynical world.

As this guy at the party was honest enough to admit, huge salaries are not a reliable measure of a job's value to society. Most of these women are actively redefining success on their own terms. Several have needed to free themselves from conventional career path thinking and invent job categories that better suit them and their purposes. "Choosing not to be a pulpit rabbi was very difficult," Mychal Springer told me, "because at first I didn't even have a concept of what making it would look like. But ultimately it was very liberating because I make it the way I make it, and that's making it." In other words, she uses her own standards to define and measure herself.

For many of these leaders, "making it" means knowing that they play a direct role in achieving tangible results on significant public issues. Laura Jervis finds it gratifying to provide housing and employment for a population that has special difficulty finding both: "For me, satisfaction comes not only from creating housing for people and making sure they have safe and quality services, but also in the numbers of jobs we've created, and the opportunities for neighborhood people who have grown." Since residents tend to stay a long time, Laura has the additional satisfaction of being able to witness their growth and increased sense of well-being.

Another leader spoke of the satisfaction that comes with being an entrepreneur and succeeding in uncharted territory. "We did lots of things that people said could never be done. We formed a huge organization that basically fights every year for an alternate budget for the city, and they're still in place." One leader set up the first "alternative to jail program" in New York City. Others cited a variety of ways that the holding environments they have created are making systemic as well as direct service differences: providing hospitality and safety, creating alternative models, influencing legislative change, galvanizing diverse people around a common cause, being the epicenter for ever-widening circles of change.

For Joan Campbell, "making a difference" means being a viable actor in world affairs: "I guess for me the greatest satisfaction is I feel like I'm part of my age. All of my life I wanted to be part of the society in which I lived, to know it, to feel it firsthand. I'm a participator in life. I'm not a watcher; I'm a player!" This she told me without a shred of superiority or pride, just amazement and awe in recognition of a blessing that had taken her by surprise. Back when she was still the traditional wife of a corporate executive in Cleveland, Ohio, she knew little of being a player, but Martin Luther King Jr.'s message of nonviolent love and civil rights had awakened her to it. "The experience with King took me from what could have been a very comfortable life to something that was far more confrontational with our society than I ever thought it would be when I was in college and thinking about what I might do with my life. . . . So I traded the predictable for the challenging and I don't think my life's ever been boring since! And, it had everything to do with practicing what I believed."

A Sense of Calling

In combination, practicing what you believe and having the conviction that it makes a meaningful difference adds up to a sense of calling. These women are finally not overcome by the draining dynamics of their work because in some larger sense they feel they are doing what they are meant to do. What a gift this is when so many people around us feel disconnected and ill at ease with their life's work. When I asked this group of women if the work was a sacrifice, they countered with powerful accounts of what vocation means to them. Echoing from one to the next is the underlying sense that these women have found their niche, their own particular way of serving the common good. As Mindy Fullilove framed it for me:

> I just feel like I'm supposed to be doing this. I feel quite driven to it by some inner force. In the moments when I feel like I'm doing what I'm supposed to do, I feel very good. The rest of the time I try to get the obstacles out of the way so that I can do what I'm supposed to be doing. I hate the obstacles [like fundraising] but the work itself is no sacrifice at all.

Others used words like passion, joy, integration, purpose, no choice, living in relation to God. Said one:

> I'm doing exactly what I want to do. There's really no sacrifice. It's a passion, despite the fact that the Jewish community is often a community that embarrasses me instead of makes me proud. I just think that Judaism could be something that is really worth celebrating, something that could so inform lives, and I believe women are the ones to make it so.

And another:

> At this point in my life, my work is certainly a calling. By that I mean that I have a sense that my person and my practice are really integrated, and that I bring a sense of purpose to everything that I do, both personal and professional, and that it's about living in relation to God, living with a sense of life being a fragile, sacred gift.

One of the Christian leaders saw it through the lens of Scripture:

I have always taken the passage of Luke dead to heart: "The spirit is upon me to preach good news to the poor." I believe that was indeed the description of Jesus' vocation and therefore ours — the church's and each of ours. I feel very strongly about the church being a place where we nurture and care for one another, but we also empower and strengthen people to go out into the hurt of the world. There's just no question in my mind about that.

These words speak for themselves. There is no doubt that a key reason these women have sustained their work over the long haul is that they are fully engaged with vital work that they feel called to accomplish. They feel connected to something larger than themselves — to what some called the energy and purposes of God — and this they experience as a blessing.

Seamlessness:
A Feminist Ethic of Connection

It was Laura Jervis who used a word that I feel captures the most appealing quality of these women's lives: seamlessness. It is a word that connotes wholeness and interconnection, not fracture. Laura used it to characterize how the pieces of her own life — professional, personal, and spiritual — are all intertwined.

My life on the West Side is really life in community. There is a sense of seamlessness to it ... which I sometimes resent a little bit because sometimes you feel you can't escape ... but most of the time I think it's the right way to live. But it is a kind of public life ... it's the community board, it's the churches and several of the synagogues, it is the WSFSH community ... and it's really all one.

Describing the exhilaration of feeling that her public and private life is of a piece, another leader told me, "I have a sense that my person and practice are really integrated and that I bring a sense of purpose to everything that I do, both personal and professional, and that it's about living in relation to God, with a sense of life being a really fragile, sacred gift."

As Laura reveals, living seamlessly entails its own tensions and challenges, but on balance she affirms that "my better self thinks it's the right way to live." She is quick to point out that by saying so, she intends no judgment toward those who do not choose to live this way. She simply attests that it allows her to live more authentically and to avoid the energy drain that maintaining compartments usually requires.

Laura's comments crystallized for me a characteristic common to all the women I interviewed: they all hold a feminist ethic of connection. For them, living a seamless life means trying to pull things together, link disparate parts, transcend boundaries, make connections — in short, to seek and value interrelationship. It entails acting in the world in harmony with one's deepest beliefs and feeling that public and private cohabitate the same continuum. This, for them, is the only way to live with integrity, to live in accordance with the nature of the world.

Bridging Boundaries and Classic Dichotomies

While many people go through life assuming the boundaries resulting from social norms are pretty much fixed, these women questioned our norms and took steps to alter them. Often this took the form of building bridges or avenues of connection between people and realms usually kept separate. For instance, these women's ethic of connection reveals itself in their emphasis on bringing people together across lines of difference. The holding environments they have created deliberately gather in people others have shunned or neglected. Their staffs and boards are purposely diverse in ethnicity, class, and faith tradition.

They do this not out of some desire to merely appear politically correct, but out of a sense that they are crafting a more authentic replica of who we collectively are — that, finally, Life is more about relation than separation. As Connie Baugh framed it, "God is a God of relation. . . . I think the most authentic spirit of God is among us and between us. That's why I believe so strongly in bridging and in community."

Connie's vision of wholeness relies on dialogue — on two-way flow — between the haves and the have-nots. Each party has something to offer and something to receive. Other leaders work with this dynamic as well: connecting people in need with those who have resources but no sense of purpose; AIDS victims with nurturing people and food that might have gone to waste; people in political power with underserved constituencies; or an unconscious public with startling information about the death penalty or ongoing violence toward women.

Other leaders devote themselves to bridging what they consider to be false dichotomies in the social realm, such as sacred versus secular or private versus public. Helen Hunt, who has recently outlined in *Faith and Feminism*[35] her desire to create a more vigorous alliance for change by healing the divide between secular feminists and feminists whose roots are religious or spiritual, told me:

> People may think the women's movement is secular, but I think the women's movement is about liberating the human spirit, and that to me makes it a spiritual work. . . . We've been in dialogue around the idea that maybe secular and spiritual are really false dichotomies, that there's a lot more overlap between what many people might label and artificially segment into either a spiritual or secular camp.

For those who consider the separation of church and state highly significant, these women leaders challenge its traditional interpretation as they begin to play with the concept of how progressive religious values can impact the public arena. A few said outright that the current insistence on separation makes no sense to them. "How can I say I believe in God," one asked, "and then get up and make a decision that's political without God still being there with me? I can't separate the two because both are who I am." Another stressed that her religious beliefs themselves do not provide for separation.

> I don't have religious beliefs that are separate from my under-standing of community and the world. I don't have some set of private religious beliefs. I was never given that orientation. In a way, my mind-set is a little more Jewish than Christian. I think it's more a sense of political good than private moral superiority that has always been the thrust of my faith.

Though this leader is Christian in background, she feels an affinity for the Jewish teaching about *tikkun olam,* or the ongoing "repair of the world" and says it articulates how her faith naturally takes the form of public work.

Another leader pointed to Jesus himself as one who enacted an ethic of seamlessness, revealing that faith flows back and forth between solitude and community, reflection and action:

> I see Jesus as the one who is faithful, who lived in commu-nity, who worked among the people, who dragged his tired self through the streets, but at the same time he could always find time for the Garden at Gethsemane. He always went off to pray, to be strengthened and have solitude.

Linda Tarry-Chard grew up in a Pentecostal church which empha-sized the indwelling of the Holy Spirit rather than more obviously activist pursuits. She retains that inwardly focused piety today, but couples it with activism in South Africa and other social and eco-nomic initiatives. "It's a wonderful combination," she tells me. "It's not throwing the baby out with the bath; it's more like changing the water."

Others felt that a natural link between church and state is forged by a concern for the "common good."

> I see the connection between religion and the public domain as being through the common good — this respect for human life across the board, all of us. And so religion is going to be the thing that's going to get you into who's suffering in the family, who's left out. We've got to go to those people, we've got to be there for them ... and that gets you involved in justice.

What we see in these examples is that bridging is not so much an architectural feat as it is a perceptual one. These women treat boundaries as being permeable. Trusting a more fluid mode, they allow imagery from one side of the membrane to wash through to the other, where it casts things there in a new light. For example, Laura Jervis found it identified her contribution best if she thought of her secular organization more as her parish with herself as the spiritual center. Henna Hahn shaped her non-profit organization around the metaphor of a family in which she and the clients were sisters and God was the mother. And though Connie Baugh recognized the practical need for two distinct organizations — a secular one called Justice Works to offer policy advocacy and the Church of Gethsemane to offer spiritual sustenance — she also felt so strongly that they be linked that she formalized it in their bylaws, creating a joint governance structure. "I wanted to make it a holistic venture," she told me, "rather than violate my basic principles and allow an artificial split between the secular and the religious."

A Vision of Society

In fact, I realized that these women practice an ethic of connection because it is central to their visions of society at its best. They experience their work as a calling because they feel that in doing it, they are acting in alignment with the unfolding energy of Spirit. They know that neither they nor society are fully integrated organisms as they now stand, but they sense that the wholeness for which we hunger lies in the direction of some fluid and complex intertwining of related spheres. As one put it: "The more we become aware of our interdependence with one another, the more we become ready to acknowledge that we affect one another and shape one another, the stronger we will be in our private lives and in our political lives." Another stressed that an emphasis on relationship does not mean that individual differences are ignored: "A phrase that first comes to mind is 'unity within diversity.' Society does not become homogenized — far from it. People are free to be extremely individual, but in addition to becoming individual, they learn the art of connection. So that we would become a society of dialogue, mutual respect, and trust in an enlarged perspective."

These leaders affirm that just as we must learn the paradoxical feel of unity within diversity, so too we may need to recognize that wholeness is a state of being which somehow unfolds at the permeable intersection of the personal and the collective. All of this will take extraordinary effort and love in the decades to come.

> It's very hard work. No one can do it by themselves and have a whole life. I think society works best when people live in community, and those communities are all circles, interlocking somehow. We need each other. Wholeness does not depend on achievement or ability, but on acceptance. It's more than tolerance. It's valuing and loving each person for who they are.

By holding the value of seamlessness, these women offer a compelling alternative to the norm of compartmentalization. They have found ways to follow a primary urge to embody their core values in every arena of their lives. Most considered their core values to be grounded in faith. Maintaining a coherence between belief and action is their definition of living with integrity, and this they highly prize.

It affords them the energy, hope, and sense of meaning which keeps them going. If their visions of society at its best are accurate, it may offer us all a better quality of life. But does this model of living violate the principle of the separation of church and state? Especially in our current era when we are so acutely aware of the dangers of religiously informed action, how can such a model be trustworthy?

Honoring the Church-State Membrane

The separation clause was designed to prevent any one religious perspective from becoming so aligned with government that there was, in effect, a state religion. The underlying motive was to ensure religious freedom — a goal I fully support. Yet, the way these women bring their faith into the public arena does not make me uncomfortable the way much of the activity of the Religious Right does. To be sure, this may in part be because they swim in the same politically and theologically progressive stream as do I. But there is more to it than that.

Although many of these leaders act from a deeply held faith, they also think critically about religion and religious institutions. They are aware of the incredibly positive power of religion to support and motivate, but are equally cognizant of its potential to alienate and divide, or to maintain an unjust status quo. They want to avoid misusing religion and religious language.

Second, they are as deeply committed to inclusiveness and diversity as they are to their own kind. They are neither supersessionist (my way is the best and right way) nor triumphalist (my religion can trump yours). Regardless of any particular sectarian beliefs they may hold, they are not preoccupied with converting people to their own way of believing. They appreciate a genuine pluralism and are finding ways to incorporate that value into their work. Not one of them requires allegiance to a particular catechism before offering food to a hungry person. Mychal Springer, a rabbi, sings in the gospel choir at the hospital. Laura Jervis, a Presbyterian minister, finds solace in the

Catholic Mass. Lee Hancock is open to varied manifestations of the divine, including those of the Goddess tradition and Voodoo.

Finally, their work is grounded in the particular. These leaders do not preach grand, fixed principles to be applied according to the letter of the law in all circumstances. Their systemic theories and policies grow out of the accumulated wisdom of responding to specific cases of human relationship and need. This grounding in the particular serves as a safeguard against self-righteous dogmatism and helps keep these leaders sympathetic, authentic, and humble.

I believe that we are not well served by the current popular interpretation of the separation clause which insists that religion has no place in the public realm. Religion and faith can still be a source of moral authority in the shared communal debate about "the common good." A full-scale retreat of the religious voice from the public arena leaves an untenable vacuum that cannot be filled by secular humanism. If all of the public religious voice is ceded to the Religious Right, then the perspective on moral issues is skewed. Having a single dominant religious voice in the public arena is the very situation that the separation of church and state was meant to prevent. Progressive religious voices must be part of the dialogue, adding richness, depth, and alternative interpretations of truth to the mix.

Some may feel that secular humanism can offer this counterbalancing perspective. I think not, though I affirm its important place in the wider debate. One of Henna Hahn's metaphors sheds lights in this regard. When she described the healing of the women at the Rainbow Center, she attributed 30 percent of their healing to reconnecting with a sense of home (through Korean food and culture), 40 percent through medicine, including therapy, and the remaining 30 percent as spiritual. Extrapolating from that metaphor, I would argue that for society as a whole to heal, some force beyond human understanding comes into play. That power, which some call God, works through specific and diverse human forms and will take up residence in that public space, try as we might to separate it out. The progressive women religionists in this book show us how religion can best be used to bind up the wounds of society, how we can ensure that no one be left behind.

The implications of living a seamless life are immense. If life is truly of a piece, there can be no boundaries between public and private, between people, between classes, between church and state. If life is of a piece and lived with love, then there is no escape from anyone's suffering or wrongdoing. Justice must apply to all. Certainly this way of living is not the exclusive domain of women, but what we can glimpse in these leaders' examples is the revolutionary power of a feminine ethic of connection. When relationship is valued over separateness, or collective action is trusted more so than individual achievement and competitiveness, a different world begins to take form.

Chapter 8

A PALIMPSEST OF FORCES

It is hard to argue with a seamless life. Who would not want one? It is as if these women have figured out the secret of life — or at least the secret of *their* lives. It may not look like what most of us call success, but it sure sounds like it. They seem to have all the important things aligned — living out their deepest values, making a difference in society, feeling whole at home and at work. How did they do it? How did these women find their way to radically full employment — a rich deployment of heart, mind, body, and soul?

I asked them. At the same time, I looked at my own life and thought about what moved me to make the choices I have. Here is what I found. There is a phrase we trot out about achievers: "They could have done anything they wanted in life." As if they have limitless choices. As if whatever careers society currently considers most lucrative and powerful are theirs for the taking.

But the fact is, having a seamless life is not about limitless choices. It is about narrowing the choices — having the courage and conviction to say "no" to all the seductive yet ill-fitting scenarios about how to spend one's life and "yes" only to the seamless one — the one that aligns one's core values with one's actions in the world. There is surprisingly little choice involved. Instead, when such people talk of finding their niche — their vocation — they say things like, "Well, I couldn't not do it."[36]

Couldn't not. Saying "yes" actually involves saying "no" twice in a row. And here we find the essence of a resistance faith — saying no to inertia and fear and yes to agency and transformation. No to dehumanizing behaviors, no to the status quo which tolerates them, and yes to the greater realization of justice. "Couldn't not" means having an urge to respond that cannot be denied. Practicing a resistance faith also means having a resistance definition of societal success — measuring it not by gross national product or the bottom line but by equal access to "hearth, heart, grail, and soul" (see chapter 2). Successful people and successful organizations are those which help make these life essentials available to all. Power is living a life of integrity, understanding that all the threads of your past come together in the current moment, in this work that you feel compelled to do on behalf of your own and other souls.

So if we want to understand the secret of these women's lives, we need to know what moved them, over the years, to say "yes" and "no." We need to try to see how the many strands of influence and experience in each woman's life gradually evolved into work, a worldview, and a way of being she recognized as uniquely and necessarily her own.

An image that holds this idea of formation for me is the palimpsest — a piece of vellum or parchment which has been written upon many times, and within which traces of the earlier layers can still be discerned. It was the earlier layers of these women's lives that I wanted to reconstruct, so that I could trace how the cumulative effect showed through in their current work and convictions. As with palimpsests, some of the tracings in all our lives remain unrecognizable. The question of formation will always be part mystery, and seemingly the product of an unnamable number of moments, meetings, and synchronicities. But there are threads that stand out, moments and messages we continually recall, experiences that undeniably build upon one another to narrow us into the fullness of our particular calling. Working on these women leaders' stories has prompted me to reflect on how this has been true for me.

A Woman's Power to Heal the World

For as long as I can remember, I've been fascinated with why some people respond to suffering and injustice while others seem not to notice it. The roots of this defining question stretch back to my childhood in Louisville, Kentucky in the 1950s and 1960s. My father was a seminary professor of Old Testament; my mother a lay leader in the Presbyterian church. Some of my earliest memories are of accompanying them in civil rights marches, feeling the press of adult bodies all around me. I was small, but unafraid, because I felt part of something big and beneficent. I vividly recall the pained way my father stood one day in our living room, recalling a time from his own youth when he watched a black man, wrongfully accused, get dragged behind a car in the square of Wilmington, North Carolina, until the body was nearly unrecognizable — pinpointing for us the wellspring of his own commitment to justice. He traveled to the Middle East when I was one and thereafter immersed himself in the religious aspects of the Israeli-Palestinian conflict and the possibilities for interreligious dialogue.

In retrospect, I realize that my parents did not shield me from the reality of evil, but rather included me in their mature struggles against it. When I was nine, a sabbatical of my father's took us to Göttingen, Germany, for a year where we rented an apartment from Dietrich Bonhoeffer's twin sister, Sabina, and her husband, Gerhard Leibholz. I heard how Bonhoeffer, a Lutheran pastor and one of the founders of the Confessing Church, had been a leader in the resistance movement against Hitler, even to the point of participating in a plot to assassinate him. For this, Bonhoeffer was later executed. When we visited memorials in the former concentration camps, the evidence of evil seemed truly overwhelming, but equally powerful were the messages that people had courageously countered it out of a conviction that every life is of inestimable value.

Another key piece of my story were models and messages about the potential of women's leadership to change organizations and respond to societal problems. My mother did not think of herself as a feminist, but she functioned as one. When I, at thirteen, was just beginning to explore womanhood, she was becoming the first woman elder in our church. The day of her election brought bitter fighting, tears, and Bible-thumping from those who thought a woman should remain silent in church and have her sphere of influence carefully circumscribed. Though a few left the church over the decision, I sensed that we were more whole as a community because she had been willing to challenge and cross that circumscribed line.

Because of the nature of this church, the religious messages I received growing up were mixed, captured in the difference between singing "Nearer My God to Thee" in the pews and "We Shall Overcome" in the streets. These were the seeds of my own yes and no ambivalence about organized religion. In Bonhoeffer and my parents, I saw evidence of the provocative, confrontational nature of religious conviction, even in the pursuit of peace. This marriage of activism and faith energized me. By contrast, the institutional church seemed rather tame and enclosed, more interested in form and maintenance. (Over time, of course, I realized that these activities are part of a continuum, both necessary for the feeding of the faithful.)

In college I returned to Germany as part of a seminar on intentional communities and the movement to resist Hitler during World War II. There I met another powerful woman, Frau Vera von Trott, then in her eighties, who had probably never heard the word feminism, yet, like my mother, embodied it. Her brother, Adam, had been killed for his resistance activities. Instead of marrying and raising a family of her own, she had taken her family's wealth and ancestral lands to found a religious community (Imshausen) to shelter children orphaned during the war. When I visited, the community had expanded its activities to include building alliances with Christians behind the Iron Curtain. She insisted to those of us gathered around her: "Women have a special role in healing the world." It was clear that Frau Vera had formed a holding environment with Imshausen — part shelter and refuge, part incubator of a peaceful society without walls of division.

My own search for a way to be publicly active with my faith led me to seminary, parish ministry, and eventually to the world of theological education. It was in seminary that I was introduced to Jung's interpretation of alchemy and Winnicott's concept of holding environment, now cornerstones in my understanding of how to alleviate suffering and injustice. Alchemical imagery affirms that "the work of great value" begins by moving toward all that is dark and rejected, instead of wishing it away or splitting it off. There a treasure lies, provided we offer hospitality to what we find there and recognize it as some aspect of ourselves, personally and collectively.

These memories and images have had a kind of magnetism in my life, attracting analogous experiences, drawing me more deeply into questions of activism and prophetic faith. It is a force that does not rest. Twenty years after seminary, I discovered I "couldn't not" study these women leaders who had caught my attention. Though I did not realize it at the outset, my fascination with their commitments was an alchemy working within me, carrying me toward the next leap of my career — the co-founding of Face to Face — a clear echo of my father's concern to sponsor peace through interreligious dialogue.

Patterns of Formation

How did I come to be who I am? My parents' commitments to an activist faith that takes risks on behalf of a greater good. The vivid evidence of the Holocaust. Stories of faithful people counteracting immense suffering. Education that met me on my growing edge, giving me a framework within which all questions and doubts were honored and critical analysis was welcomed. Imagery that named new truths. Letting the unrelenting magnetism guide me.

I was curious to see what highlights and turning points the women leaders might name. As I interviewed, I asked them open-ended questions to avoid imposing my preconceptions.

- Growing up, who were the most influential people in your life? Who really saw you?

- Did religion or a church or synagogue play a part in your family life growing up?

- How did you get the message that involvement in public life or repairing the world is an important life pursuit? How did you know you could do this?

- Were there any breakthrough experiences or critical incidents that you feel were especially formative?

- How do you now connect your deepest convictions about life with your public work to change the world?

My questions, in part, were influenced by patterns of formation identified in two studies which preceded mine. The first, *The Altruistic Personality,* conducted by Samuel and Pearl Oliner,[37] was designed to explore the origins of altruism, especially as it manifested in people who rescued Jews during the Holocaust. A key question they hoped to answer was: what motivates or allows people to risk their lives to prevent the suffering of those who are "other"? Their findings concluded that the rescuers had learned values from their families of origin that included empathy and caring, generosity and hospitality, and a sense of belonging to a larger human family for which they bore some responsibility. The families had also given the rescuers a sense of internal authority that allowed them ultimately to override external authority (government policy during the Holocaust, for example), even at great personal risk.

The second study, conducted by Laurent A. Parks Daloz and colleagues, looked more broadly at people whose lives were devoted to "the common good."[38] This implies having a vision of the interconnected whole of life, superseding personal gain; it reflects global concern and an appreciation for pluralism and diversity. Although some postmodern thinkers would argue that there is no such thing as the common good in the context of increasing diversity and complexity, I maintain that there is still a shared public space that bears the imprint of our best efforts at justice, equality, and peace. The book, *Common Fire,* discusses the key formative factors which appeared repeatedly in the lives of those studied: messages and models from family, the influence of religious tradition, personal experiences of suffering and marginalization, engagement with people from backgrounds and cultures different from their own, relationships with mentors and role models, and the impact of historical eras such as world wars, the Depression, or the 1960s.

In many respects, the women I interviewed confirmed the findings about formation that both of these studies offer. I will review them briefly here before turning to some specific stories from the women leaders that extend these findings.

Family

In the midst of family, we are infused with the most enduring images of how the world is and what our role within it might be. It is here that we first learn the vocabulary of relationship: to whom and to what are we connected, indebted, accountable, loyal? If suffering is experienced, how is it received? How is adversity handled, and success defined? Around the dinner table, we sense whether we are heard or not, seen or not, a respected life player or not. The answers have much to do with whether our parents, or the surrogate mothers and fathers who bring us into being in those early years, have sorted out the yeses and nos of their own lives well. In their commitments, we get our first glimpse of what is worth giving one's life for. In their brokenness, and how they persevere with it, we gather strands of compassion, rage, forgiveness, and resolve toward a better way. Everything about the way they move through life seeps into us and becomes our first conviction about how the world is. In the palimpsest of life, family is indelible.

These women heard messages from their parents about sharing with others, midwifing justice, enacting their beliefs. "Living beyond oneself," Laura Jervis's grandmother told her, was the purpose of life. Mothers enmeshed in poverty nevertheless demonstrated to their daughters, "You have plenty to give." When I asked Linda Tarry-Chard how she knew she could do her diversity work, transforming hearts one at a time and in a gathering wave, she said: "Because they all told me I could. Since it was expected of me, and I was doing it as far back as I can remember, there was never any doubt that I wouldn't or couldn't. That message was always conveyed: You can, you should, you will."

Religion

Religion takes the dramas and questions of the family microcosm and projects them onto the big screen. It turns "what do you want to be when you grow up?" into "what is the purpose of human existence and how do I fit into that larger purpose?" It casts the brokenness and shortcomings of our family lives as part of the great Story of the suffering of a people, longing for transformation and redemption. Religion, when it works well, confirms that though we are small, we are part of something big — a force of spirit with a connective or binding power that can gather up suffering and transmute it toward wholeness, over and over again. Religion offers images of realities beyond our conscious grasp but within our intuitive reach. It challenges us to live faithfully in the space between, working toward the interconnectedness of all things and a shared vision of a more just world.

By belonging to religious communities, many of the women I interviewed felt the seamless connection between faith and public work. It was here that they began to understand that living a life of integrity meant acting with others in concert with one's deepest beliefs. "I have never seen faith apart from public life," one said simply. Sitting in church, these women learned inclusiveness — that the human family was broad, that all were children of God, and that the gifts of all were worthy and necessary to advance grassroots and collaborative efforts. For some, the religious community provided an environment of warmth and acceptance, characteristics that the leaders often replicated in the holding environment nature of the organizations they founded. Some of the women experienced religious communities whose emphasis on hospitality and nurture was linked with a broadening and challenging vision: that the human family and world to which they were connected were much more diverse than they had known.

It was to a large extent from their respective religious traditions that these women learned that making a difference in the world is not just a matter of being charitable, it necessarily involves critical thinking and analysis of the underlying causes of systemic injustice. Some, like me, got a sense of the countercultural role of religion and the church to transform society, to make change, to repair the world, to stir things up, to resist the status quo, to take risks.

Being Marginal

The experience of being marginal is a powerful teacher, and the lessons learned particularly relevant to the make-up of progressive social entrepreneurs. There are different kinds of marginality lessons, depending on what has made a person feel marginal and whether they feel alone with it.

The *Common Fire* team speaks of two types of marginality: vulnerability-based and value-based. The first results from oppressions, poverty, illness, disability. The second has a more positive cast and is about feeling special or set apart because of values one holds, usually in company with self-selected others, as in political or religious affiliation. Both mark a person as "other." The gift of either form is that being "other" places a person on the edges of a group or phenomenon, and from there one can see and assess its behavior better than when one is in the midst of it. Distance yields perspective.

Being "other" in a positive way creates a sense of belonging and a value-based identity that enhances one's sense of agency in the world. Because it supports adhering to alternative values within a non-supporting milieu, value-based marginality particularly sponsors the ability to resist the dominant ethos.

Being "other" in the more vulnerable sense involves suffering — feelings of being odd, unacceptable, unworthy, dysfunctional, even less than human. Such experiences can be crippling. But when there are mitigating factors which help them to be experienced as meaningful or constructive, they can be also be the source of insight into human evils and systemic injustices. And there is certainly truth to the common understanding that they can become a bridge that links us to all others who suffer. Several of the women leaders suffered racism, poverty, sexism, classism, disability, and disease in ways that engendered in them a sensitivity to the suffering of whole classes of people. Instead of breaking them, their personal suffering oriented them toward areas of great need.

Experiences of both types of marginality can also develop a certain tolerance for inhabiting marginal spaces or thinking outside the box. (It must be said that despite gains in access to authority and power, being a woman in our society still puts you on the margin; adding other characteristics of marginality such as race or class means that some are doubly marginalized or more.) Nearly all of the women I interviewed are social entrepreneurs, working creatively outside the boundaries of mainstream structures and organizations.

Embracing "Other"

Throughout life we encounter people who, at least initially, seem very different from ourselves. The question is, how do we evaluate those differences? Do they make us fearful or uncomfortable? intrigued and eager to learn more? superior or inferior? If these "other people" are not "like us," do they still merit our respect, attention, and care? How does their perspective on life enhance or challenge our own? Do we even know how to relate to them on a deeper level or do we wish they did not exist?

The women leaders I interviewed demonstrated a remarkable commitment to inclusiveness, to consciously including the "other." The *Common Fire* study identified one critical formative factor shared by all of those who had this trait and worked for the common good — a transforming discovery that they held something in common even with one perceived as distinctly "other." It is these commonalities which bridge our ongoing differences, which make porous the boundary we tend to have between ourselves and others.

An experience of marginality can have this effect. As the *Common Fire* team points out, "Anthropologists have long observed that those marginal in their own group or tribe are the first to reach out to strangers."[39] When you have experienced being dismissed as "other" yet still retain a conviction about your own humanity, you have a lasting motivation to embrace the essential humanity in even the most alien stranger.

We may also learn that it is we who need this alien for the sake of our own growth and maturity, rather than the other way around. Laura Jervis, who coined for me the notion of a seamless life, was imprinted with this idea as a child. Because her father was a doctor studying mental disability, the family grew up on the grounds of a center for mentally retarded adults and children. She formed an early bond with the adults who took care of her as a child, later worked alongside them caring for children, and well appreciated their gifts. To her, they were contributing members of an extended family. It was only years later that she discovered that society at large considered them significantly dysfunctional.

We can see this ongoing appreciation for the "other" in the way the women leaders insist that their boards be diverse and that their clients participate in governance so that they will have a voice in setting the direction of their organizations. As one put it, "Dealing with people all across the political and religious spectrum has been a real challenge and a big education for me. And the ones who are most different have educated me more than anybody else. In order to understand who they are, I've had to really engage who I am in relation to them, and that has been exciting to delve into."

I refer to all senses of being marginal and embracing otherness as "Inclusiveness Lessons."

Mentors

Though our parents are given to us, for the most part it is we who choose our mentors, and as such they have particular power to focus and extend our sense of vocation. We see them up ahead of us on the path and feel fortunate to join them for a while. They seem to know the lay of the land better than we, and the best ones seem to know *us* better than we know ourselves. This quality of feeling known by a respected one is powerfully validating and often has a numinous quality to it.

Not all the women in the study named mentors, especially female ones. Helen Hunt poignantly observed of her early years, "It was a heroine wasteland out there." For some, mentors appeared at important moments to awaken them to broader issues or push them into a greater sense of their own agency. One male activist pastor was cited by several of the women leaders as having had confidence in them before they were able to have confidence in themselves: "All along he just sort of put me out front." Other mentors offered analytical tools for placing personal experience within a larger social context — a key step in the one-on-one systemic dance.

Just as important as single individuals were mentoring communities or groups of women who provided not only insight but actual coaching about women's leadership. A group of women in the African-American Pentecostal church where Linda Tarry-Chard grew up showed her how to speak and act as a leader, chair meetings, organize, galvanize, delegate, and raise money. Laura Jervis had her "cabal" of women peers who affirmed and challenged each other.

Ironically, not one leader mentioned having been encouraged early on by a pastor or rabbi or anyone else to pursue professional religious leadership, much less the public dimensions of such leadership. It may be that many of these women were simply growing up in a time when the ordination of women was relatively new or when women interested in religion might have been diverted to teaching. In fact, the idea of becoming a public religious leader was not one that would have occurred to many people growing up in the latter half of the twentieth century in America for a variety of reasons, and to a significant degree that remains so today. As a result, few of the women I interviewed were guided in this direction during their youth by parents, teachers, or mentors — which makes their emergence as leaders pursuing this kind of work all the more remarkable.

Education

Over half of the women I interviewed had some sort of advanced training, for example in seminary or rabbinical school or social work. Yet, surprisingly few cited formal education as being particularly relevant to their current work. That is, they were not explicitly taught the entrepreneurial necessities of organizational design and development, advocacy and fundraising. Several, however, did recognize that education had given them critical social analysis tools — perspectives from socio-political theory, psychology, policy-making, and theology which helped them think strategically about systemic change.

On the critical issue of developing language with which to express progressive religious insights, those with seminary or rabbinical school education seemed to have greater sensitivity and articulateness.

They learned their most vivid lessons through experiential, practical education like field work. By serving under supervision as case workers, chaplains, and prison advocates, these women got a taste for the policy issues and the real people behind them.

History Lessons — The Ethos of an Era

All of us are shaped not only by the individuals and communities around us but by the larger era and ethos in which we live. Cultural trends and preoccupations, specific historical events, and broad movements for change are the air we breathe. Some of these that were salient for the women leaders are not surprising: feminism, the Civil Rights movement, and the 1960s more generally.

Feminism in particular deserves elaboration. Many of their organizations are shaped by articulated feminist values of compassion, nurture, inclusiveness, collaboration, and mutual empowerment; several seek to empower or advocate for women and girls. Many of the leaders spoke of strong or "iconoclastic" mothers who were either proto-feminists themselves or who made sure their daughters had the education and self-esteem to explore non-traditional roles.

Another influential historical era took me by surprise — the Holocaust. Although it has been central in my own thinking, I was unprepared for how often the women referred to it, totally unprompted by me. Over half of them did so, Christians and Jews alike. It seemed to serve as a talisman of our capacity to treat the "other" as less than human, and it helped them articulate questions about the human capacity for good and evil and complicity in the structures of injustice. These questions were not merely of historical interest for them, but very much related to analysis of the contemporary situation. How do we stay alert in our own time to avoid holocausts? As Annie Bovian warned, "Our society is so permeated by racism that most people can see it and not feel like there's anything wrong with it. In New York, 95 percent of those who are incarcerated are people of color. How far are we here in the United States from what happened in Germany?" Faced with systemic oppressions, will we be complicit or take the necessary risks?

Finally, a broad cultural phenomenon that is central to these women's development is the increased consciousness about religious pluralism that has marked the last decades of the twentieth century, along with a movement toward secularism (see chapter 1). This is the religious terrain that began shaping these women leaders while they were in college, graduate school, or very early in their careers. Today, it is the context which their faith-based leadership must honor and address. And it is precisely around this point that the women I interviewed become a special case in the broader study of formation which *Common Fire* initiated.

The Making of a Progressive Entrepreneur

While these women's stories certainly confirm the findings on formation described by the *Common Fire* team, they also offer an opportunity to look more closely at religious formation per se. In interviewing these women leaders, I specifically hoped to better understand how they developed into progressive religious leaders. How did they learn to practice what I call "resistance faith"? What clues would I find in their backgrounds which might explain how they learned to treat outcasts with dignity and hospitality, or how they cultivated both the chutzpah and moral conviction to take on the evils embedded in our social systems? What taught them to say both "yes" and "no" to organized religion — to tap its strengths while challenging its hypocrisies and compromises? How, for instance, did they learn to move beyond the parochialism of sectarian religious thinking and instead be "converted" to pluralism?

In retrospect, I realized that this would involve understanding how they developed what I call an "alchemical imagination" — their penchant for seeing the possibilities for transformation that exist even within the darkest conditions. There were also their remarkable convictions about inclusiveness and seamlessness to account for. And, in focusing exclusively on women leaders, I hoped to surface some patterns that might be especially relevant to the way women help heal the world.

Here are four of stories which illustrate the rich interplay of forces at work in the making of progressive spiritual entrepreneurs. Pondering them will begin to yield an answer to the tantalizing question of how to cultivate resistance faith.

Learning and Teaching That Others Are Kin

Seeing us all as children of God — each with different gifts. That's just such a wonderful message to learn early on, because it makes you fully accept, respect, and feel at one with everyone.

— Linda Tarry-Chard

Linda's founding of Project People, the economic development project involving black dolls (see chapter 3), cannot be understood apart from the inescapable reality of being a black person in this society. As Linda told me:

> In this skin, in this lifetime, being a woman from a black culture and all that that culture teaches me has very much shaped who I am and how I perform or how I function or how I exist. I think in terms of how one navigates struggles and hard times, not having the luxury of disposable income, coming from a people who were

denied education, denied access to power. This means how we cope with problems and struggles is internalized, is different from someone else, who has been given other options. That has made me who I am.

Linda was born and raised in a borough of New York City in a lower-middle-class family. Her earliest sense of "tribe" came from being part of a very close nuclear family with many women mentors, including her mother, grandmothers, and the community of the Black Pentecostal church. These two families — home and church — voiced messages that still shape her life: "God has blessed you, so you may bless others," "giving is being," and "everyone has a cross to bear." The latter was the great leveler, affirming that regardless of life circumstances, no one goes unscathed. Yet, the unconditional love she enjoyed from this intimate group of African-American family and friends offered a safe cocoon of belonging and identity — a critical counterbalance to racism.

> It was wonderful because it made me feel very loved as far back as I can remember — very blessed. That's a wonderful way of being — just never alone. Whatever it is you need, someone will provide it. That's a very comforting sense. You don't have to even think about being rejected by someone else if all you want is here.

Linda explained that being in this community was like taking Management 101 from pre-school onward. "I knew how to conduct meetings by the time I was four, probably, because my mother was President or Treasurer of this or that committee and was having meetings all the time." These leadership lessons by osmosis were coupled with the message that Linda not only could, but should make a difference with her life — that her gifts were needed and wanted. In fact, the church's teaching on discovering gifts was to become a cornerstone of Linda's perspective on diversity.

I learned a very important message in the church — at home as well — and that is everyone has a gift. And, you see, in the church you can demonstrate that. If you can sing you're in the choir. If you can't sing, then you're an usher. Well, if you can't stand on your feet and do that, then you raise money. The list went on, and that's just such a wonderful message to learn early on, because it makes you fully accept, respect, and feel at one with everyone. So, "we haven't found what yours is yet, but we will — before this meeting is over you're going to have a job." It's just a given that you come with a gift.

This is a legacy which Linda has carried forward into her own work, ensuring that everyone's gifts are tapped for the task at hand.

Linda's early cocoon of support cracked open when her father, determined to provide a better education for his children, moved the family to a predominantly Jewish neighborhood. To her surprise, Linda discovered kinship across difference.

Here were people not only of a different color but a different faith. I learned fairly early on that there was an empathy. Jews weren't like other white people. . . . Eventually I learned about the Holocaust. They understood persecution; they understood being ostracized; they understood being outside. So there was a safety being with them that you would not necessarily have with other white people. So, my affinity to Jews, which is very apparent in my adult life now, started at an early age.

Over time, these sustained relationships with Jews opened a window to shared empathy with other marginalized people. These experiences began breaking down the categories of white and black, gradually enlarging her sense of who belonged. Over forty years later, it would be a call from the American Jewish Committee and a cup of tea with a

South African Jewish social worker that would set Linda on the path to founding Project People. Linda's first experience of being "the other" herself also had lasting effects.

> African-Americans — no matter how old they are — you ask them when was the first time they ever had a racist incident and they can recall it, quite vividly, graphically. I was about seven, and it was the first time that I was rejected and knew it was because of my skin color. I was called a nigger. This was by a little girl who had moved into the building whose family was Irish Catholic.

Her mother's response was something like my father taking me to the memorial at a concentration camp. Here beside a girl too young to understand stood a mature adult, acknowledging the reality of what took place, and offering a way forward.

> I didn't fully comprehend what was going on at the time, but my mother handled it so gently, lovingly, and wonderfully, so that it wasn't a scarring moment. I remember her looking at me with pain on her face, and then going to the silverware drawer. She took out two spoons, one tarnished and one stainless steel and brilliantly polished. . . . She said, "All through life there will be people like this, some who are pure and some who are tarnished, like this spoon, and you must know the difference, and you will stay away from people who are like that. It's just who they are and what they are." She didn't in any way project upon a lifetime of incidents by saying, "All white people are like this and you need to stay away from them."

Years later, Linda was also confronted with rejection by her home church. At eighteen, she had married an older man, had a son, but soon divorced — a move not countenanced by the Pentecostal church.

Suddenly Linda became "the other" to the very group that had once insulated her. It was a moment of growth and individuation. Linda, who had learned her inclusiveness lessons well, began to question some of the values of the Pentecostal church.

Having experienced the value of a strong community, she chose to "give something back" by doing special education, social service, and community work in Harlem. Gradually, she felt herself "back stepping into the church." She remarried, had another child, and eventually decided to go to seminary, choosing to be ordained in the United Church of Christ, a denomination "with a history of upholding the oppressed" and one which more explicitly emphasized the value of public work.

She told me that rather than discarding her heritage from the Pentecostal church, she feels she has complemented its strengths with new understandings.

> My early religious training was that God is within, an ever-present friend...but there was no nurturing of the reaching out. I've taken that and now coupled it with what I've learned by experience, what I've learned in my academic pursuits, and I reach out.

Jesus, in her view, is one who tried to change the environment wherever he was. She too would like to be this kind of transforming presence. "Being involved with people who I feel have been marginalized, I like to think of that as part of who I am. Seeing us all as children of God — each with different gifts — but all equals in the sight of God." She has been a boundary crosser throughout her career, whether working with disadvantaged youth, conducting diversity training in corporate settings, serving as associate minister at Riverside Church in New York City, or heading up Project People Foundation. When I asked her to name her greatest satisfactions, she said:

It would be bringing together diverse groups of people around a common good, a common cause. And not bringing them together without meaning, bringing them together for a deeper meaning. But at each one of those career junctures I think in some way I have transformed or changed a life. And not only for black people. Every one of those commitments in some way touched on people outside of my own ethnic group, and I think that's important. Transformation should be contagious.

The founding of Project People Foundation, an economic development program for women in South Africa and the United States, brought together all of the influences and commitments of her life — a belief in the possibility of transformation in the face of the systemic oppression of apartheid, and a conviction that diverse people working together can achieve justice.

Convinced That Transformation Happens

So much of one's life experience would point to the fact that things don't change, that change is so difficult, and sometimes dangerous. But that's where faith comes in. — Jan Orr Harter

Jan Orr-Harter describes herself as being most at home when she's moving across barriers. She says she's been that way since she was a child, in part because of a bit of parental benign neglect.

When I was six my mother had twins, and I more or less moved across the street to a Jewish family from Englewood, New Jersey, and really grew up in their religious tradition. Spent Fridays and holidays with them, even tried to learn Hebrew. They were much more Jewish than your typical Fort Worth Jewish family. They also subscribed to the *New Yorker* magazine, which was probably the only subscription in Fort Worth, Texas in 1960. And they knew about the United Nations. So they kind of opened my eyes. They explained to me about the Holocaust. I remember standing there looking at the candles and them telling me. I just told them I was sure that they were wrong, that it could not possibly have happened. But they explained to me what had happened, and it made a deep impression on me.

At the same time I was also crossing the barrier and going down to the fundamentalist Baptist Vacation Bible School on my own initiative in the summertime. My parents didn't really know where I was, but it was an air-conditioned building and so I went. So I kind of knew those folks too.

As the eldest of five, Jan remembers having lots of freedom and independence as a child. "That certainly shaped my sense of what I can do." Her parents treated her more as an adult and included her in their own concerns. The family was active in a liberal Methodist church when she was a child, but as she became a teenager in the 1960s, her parents were asked to leave it because they had allowed the senior high fellowship to read *The Catcher in the Rye*. In response, Jan and her parents helped organize an experimental Presbyterian fellowship that met in people's houses. They studied the theologians Tillich and Niebuhr and new emerging theologies like feminist theology. With a focus on "waking the sleeping giant of the suburban church," this small community became concerned with civil rights, the Vietnam war, and local social issues.

Here we see an example of how a critique of the church can come from a deeper understanding of the church's own root message. Jan and this small community felt the suburban church had lost its inherent mission — to be wholly involved with social justice — and they set about to try to change that.

The suburban church wasn't the only giant who needed awakening. Jan saw "lots of people being transformed by this little church," including her own father.

He went from a Texas, conservative, pro-military type to somebody who was really very much against the Vietnam war and concerned about civil rights issues, served on the Human Rights Commission of Fort Worth, investigating police brutality against the black community — all through this church. And so I really saw that and got to experience some of their transformation vicariously.

Jan still points to this time as the reason for her confidence in people's capacity for change.

I think there's no point in engaging in political life, even personal life, unless you believe people can change. I mean, that's got to be a fundamental understanding of the gospel, that change is possible and that people can change. And so seeing that so close at hand sort of taught me a lot about Jesus.

This experimental church was also responsible for her conviction that faith and public life are inextricably intertwined.

You know, I have never seen faith apart from public life. I've always understood the gospel as having something to do with change in the world — that the whole surrender to Jesus had to do with his message of calling forward change.

She began to practice this credo in high school, becoming active in student government in order to work on human rights, world peace (a particular emphasis of her mother's), and addressing the environmental crisis through recycling. During this time, Cesar Chavez and Martin Luther King Jr. were important role models.

Years later, after seminary and ten years as associate minister of an urban church heavily involved in nuclear freeze initiatives, she felt called to revitalize a church with only nine members. In researching its history, she discovered a mentor of sorts — a man who, like King and

Chavez, got radicalized by taking the gospel more seriously than those
in the established church. He was Jan Hus, a Bohemian priest of the
Middle Ages who questioned the Catholic church's collusion with feu-
dal structures and sought to democratize the institution. His story is
a remarkable example of the spirit of resistance faith. Though Hus
was burned at the stake, his followers survived the Counter Refor-
mation by maintaining an underground network and were among the
first Protestants. Centuries later, in the late 1880s, their Czechoslo-
vakian descendents migrated to New York City and founded Jan Hus
Church. A central tenet was that church should remain very down-to-
earth, that there should be a close connection between religion and
practical, daily life. Even the architecture embodied this:

> They built a church that looks like a house. It doesn't look like
> something different from the rest of the world. And they called
> it "the House." They built 50 rooms for people to live in. They
> had dental clinics, work clinics, sewing classes, language classes.
> They had a lot of focus on art and physical fitness, trying to help
> the immigrant, who was basically kind of the replaceable part of
> industry, to have a better rounded, more humane life, which was
> a pretty radical notion at the turn of the century.

Remarkably progressive and theologically open for its time, the
church had women leaders and included the following in its credo:
"Do you believe that the church stays close to the poor and humili-
ated peoples of the world and never becomes a tool of oppression or
power? Do you believe we can gain wisdom from other religions?"

By reconnecting the church with its heritage, Jan developed "the
House" into a sanctuary for Salvadoran refugees and reached out to
disenfranchised groups in the immediate neighborhood. When I asked
her what she felt was at stake in her efforts, I realized that sleeping
giants were once again on her mind.

On the Upper East Side of Manhattan, in the silk stocking district, not too far from one of the poorest neighborhoods in New York, East Harlem, was there going to be a congregation that was known for reaching across barriers of rich and poor, of including people who had been excluded from the church, of continuing to hold together the spiritual, the worldly and the political in the search for justice and peace? Would there be a church on the Upper East Side of Manhattan that was focused on that understanding of Jesus, or not? That's what was at stake.

Saying Yes and No to Organized Religion

I was absolutely shocked at the quality of human life that we simply locked out. And that really started me going. — Connie Baugh

Connie Baugh, founder of a church and a criminal justice policy reform organization for women ex-prisoners, is motivated by a distinction between legalism and justice that she became sensitive to even as a child. Her uncle, an alcoholic, was in and out of jail for episodes of domestic violence. Since she knew him to be a wonderful man, she began to wonder why this was society's only response to his condition. When her father was incapacitated by a heart condition, her mother, with an eighth grade education, became the sole breadwinner for the family. She did domestic work, but also worked in the numbers racket to make ends meet. Again, the justice system came into question. "My mother was not a bad person, so what was this law that made her criminal?"

In fact, Connie sees the seeds of her own motivation as an activist and her vocation as minister as being rooted in her mother's modeling.

How did I become such an activist? My mother was always active in the church. She was an example to me of a Christian in the best sense. She understood that it wasn't just a Sunday thing, and she was extremely generous with whomever, whether we could afford to be or not. If you had two potatoes you shared one. It wasn't a debate. You didn't think about "is this the right thing to do?" It was a natural flow. And so I always knew growing up that part of my role in life was to be there for those who had less, even though we ourselves had so little. And the idea of taking seriously the political arena was implied, because, after all, we've got to make this world a better place to live. That was always taught.

But there were questions of legalism in the church as well. Connie vividly remembers the time her invalid father, as a surprise for the rest of the family, labored for hours to get dressed and come to church. Connie and her sister and mother were thrilled to see him, but it was noon by the time he arrived. When he said to the minister, "I've come for Communion," the minister said that he was too late and that next time he'd have to arrive on time. Connie, aged eight, screamed and began kicking the minister in the shins, shouting, "You're not a man of God; you're not a man of God." Her mother later let her know that though her perception was accurate, she would need to find other means of addressing the problem. Years later, she would.

This same church was the very place where Connie and her mother felt they were seen and received as whole people — a great gift, given their ongoing struggles with the shame and burden of poverty.

The church was certainly generous to us with hams and turkeys and we were grateful, but that's not why I love the church. I love the church because it was a community of people that cared for one another. One of the reasons I felt so strongly about the poor having their own church is that I learned through my childhood church — a United Methodist congregation — that everyone matters. My mother was poor — and ashamed of it — but she had the most beautiful voice in the church, and she was encouraged to share it. She had something to give and a place that would receive it. And that was critical to my mother's self-respect, and I think important in my development too.

These memories reveal that by her early teenage years, Connie was already practicing a discerning resistance faith—saying "no" to legalism devoid of compassion, "no" to false men of God, and "yes" to "Christian in the best sense."

Having experienced the healing potential of religious community, and having been taught by her mother that education was the way out of poverty, Connie entered college and began a religious studies major. Coming from a small city environment, she considered involvement with the community a given at college in a rural setting. She discovered that in addition to the university the only other large institution in the area was a penitentiary for men and that there was no relationship between them. She spent two years trying to get the university interested in creating one. She found that though the Protestants were not interested, the Catholics on campus were. Together they established a release program so prisoners could attend classes at the university. By senior year, she was assistant teaching a religious studies course which included men from the prison. The lessons they taught her galvanized her resolve to counteract the dehumanizing experiences of prison life.

I got to know them intellectually, personally, and I was shocked. I was absolutely shocked at the quality of human life that we simply locked out. And that really started me going. I became very close friends with one of the men, learned a lot about his background, and what happens to people who end up in prison.

Sensing that there was a role for the churches to play, she decided to attend Union Seminary in New York City. She immediately got involved with the prison system on Rikers Island as part of her field study, only to find the church's response unimaginative and legalistic.

I absolutely could not believe, I couldn't fathom that we had a whole island of people who were simply locked up. It was just overwhelming to me. When I sat and heard the stories, I could only weep. I mean, my childhood was far from easy. Having grown up in enormous poverty and a lot of family violence around alcoholism, I could identify with their stories. But I also knew that the issue of race played a major role. And I also couldn't believe that the only thing the church was doing in there was preaching about how bad these people were and that they needed to repent.

Here was her small city childhood turned urban and writ large. She recalled that she was not fully conscious of the connections at the time; they would surface in flashes as she got more involved in the work. For now, she simply let her passion to transform the situation overcome the voice that was asking what "a nice, white, liberal do-gooder" could possibly do for an entire island of black and Hispanic poor people. She went to the warden and said simply, "I want to help." The warden, who became an important mentor, hooked her up with a woman in the pretrial wing who needed a court advocate. It was a match.

I had no idea what else I was going to do. I just knew when I took the job that I really loved it, that it was right. I was reading everything I could get my hands on. I made friends with attorneys so they would teach me law. I was just totally immersed and there was just no question in my mind this is where the church belonged.

Here we see the alchemist's imagination at work — her willingness, even eagerness, to immerse herself in the dehumanizing prison system. Her mother was actually horrified that she was doing so. Her dream for Connie was that she would go into business and earn lots of money.

Now she feared for her safety. Yet Connie felt she was doing precisely what her mother had always taught her — to stand up for what she believed was right. Connie decided her mother needed to meet some of the prisoners herself.

> The women were thrilled and made coffee and cookies for her. Of course, Mother became everybody's mother before she left there, and by eleven o'clock that night she was saying, "My God, these are just a bunch of poor girls that just don't have any guidance; they need some help from some caring adults."

As any alchemist can tell you, turning to meet the darkness immediately begins to transform it. It's distancing and denial that keep it dark and menacing.

At Rikers, Connie designed and directed a pre-release center for women prisoners which in three years reduced the return rate from 80 percent to 10 percent "by simply providing necessary resources inside and a connection to the community post-release." Using this as a model, she went on to found Citizen Advocates for Justice in 1978. The Church of Gethsemane came into being in 1985 in response to women ex-prisoners' need to be welcomed into a spiritual community rather than treated as social outcasts. And, in 1991, she founded Justice Works Community as a vehicle for addressing criminal justice policy issues.

All of these organizations are characterized by inclusivity — the conviction that all should be welcome in the household of God — and an appreciation for flexibility above legalism. One of the biggest obstacles in getting acceptance of the idea of a church for and by ex-prisoners was that many members of traditional congregations could not accept that felons could hold ordained positions on a level with the respected members of their own congregations. But Connie insisted that the poor had a right to be ordained and that the larger church needed to hear the voices of the poor. "And to this day, I don't care what church I serve, I will never deny someone Communion."

Over the twenty years that Connie led these organizations, people often remarked at how difficult it must be for her to work with "those people." But poor people were like home to her. "I *am* 'those people.'" Relating to wealthy people was actually the greater challenge, and she had to do it frequently when fundraising for her non-profits.

> I never thought I would resolve my own class conflicts to the point where wealthy people were individuals and people to me, rather than a class unto themselves, people I felt were so "other." . . . People often thought and they would say to me: "Oh, it must be so hard, your work must be hard." They felt it was dealing with prisoners that was hard, but it was dealing with the wealthy and sometimes self-righteous people in the churches who had no idea what poverty was or why crime could occur.

It was not until years into the work that a breakthrough came. Connie had been speaking about her work and a potential patron from a wealthy church had badgered her with questions. After a lunch break:

> The man stood up and apologized and just sobbed and said: "We have all this money, and we have no mission and no meaning, and there you are rich with life and meaning, and have no money. I don't understand why we can't work together."

In that poignant moment, the playing field was leveled. She realized that the rich could experience poverty too — poverty of meaning — and that she, despite her literal poverty, had riches to share. Now they were bound together by mutual need. She saw that she had been equally guilty of treating the rich as the other in violation of her own theological and ethical beliefs.

Now her spirituality centers on connection and bridging:

God is a God of relation. . . . I think that the most authentic spirit of God is among us and between us. That's why I believe so strongly in bridging and in making community. Once upon a time I believed that you worked with the poor and the hell with the rest. Now I believe that you must work not with the rich about the poor, not with the poor alone, but with the communities . . . and bring those communities into dialogue with each other.

Joining Progressive Values with Reclaimed Spirituality

What are you doing about poverty and inequity in the world?
— Ruth Messinger

"Is this a place where people with ideals can work?" This is the question Ruth Messinger was asking herself when she majored in Government in college. She'd chosen the major as a means of pursuing her interest in political theory, and realized in hindsight that it gave her no idea of what she'd be getting into if she held public office. That she would "learn fast on the job" some fifteen years later while serving her first term as a New York City Councilwoman and later as Manhattan Borough President.

She had been persuaded to enter the City Council race in the mid-1970s by democratic operatives on the West Side who were seeking new energy for a flagging party reform movement they had begun in the 1960s. Ruth was known at the time as someone with very grassroots politics, a passion for public education, and a commitment to diversity that she really lived.

By then, her question about idealism had evolved into: "how much and in what way can I represent the things I care about and still get something done?" When I asked what she cared about, her answer came back fast and sure: "Poverty, social justice, economic democracy, inequity, education, and jobs." Progressive values in spades. How did she have such conviction about them, especially at a time when, as she put it, "The general attitude was, and still is, that all the things that I believed in and stood for had already had their day and no one was ever going to do anything for them or about them again."

"Their day" was the era of the 1960s, when Ruth had come of age, and this had clearly shaped her thinking about public policy. But her commitment can be traced all the way back to the family dinner table. Ruth's family read and discussed three newspapers a day. Information on public issues "flew around the household nonstop."

Her mother, Marjorie, held a doctorate in philosophy, and was the first director of public relations at the newly founded Jewish Theological Seminary, whose Chancellor realized the strategic role the seminary could play in giving the new Conservative Judaism a public face. It was Marjorie's job to choose a theme, often with contemporary relevance, and explain to a lay person what Judaism's ancient texts and contemporary writings had to say about it. Ruth was her mother's proofreader, and so got early exposure to position papers on domestic violence, social injustices, and environmental concerns. "Even more than the ideas," Ruth recalls, "I remember that my mother's work was at one and the same time Jewish, relevant, and important."

In addition to holding a full-time job for nearly all of her adult life — unusual for middle class women in the 1940s and 1950s — Ruth's mother was active with several Jewish social service agencies. Ruth particularly remembers her redefining their role to extend their services beyond the Jewish community — "which is, of course, what I am doing now."

My mother was an incredible role model — for the number of things that she took on, for the ways in which she could really be seen to be living her values, and for the sense we had growing up, the true sense, that she was so different from most of the women that she knew or that we knew because she had lots more pieces in her life.

Ruth was also drawn to her maternal grandfather, a man who "clearly defined himself and his role in the world in terms of Jewish values — work for social justice, the notion of giving something back." He had been the first executive director of the New York Federation of Jewish Philanthropies and had remained a moving force in the organization for over fifty years.

Clearly, involvement with public issues and philanthropy on behalf of social justice are part of Ruth's bloodline. Another characteristic of this bloodline was a movement away from organized religion. All of Ruth's grandparents were less observant than their own parents had been and seemed to favor an assimilation stance. Ruth's parents, however, felt differently. Knowing of my interest in religious formation, Ruth recently gave me access to an article her mother had written when Ruth was a child, detailing her thinking about how to bring religious observance back into their lives in a manner which was tied to the tradition but also keyed to their modern concerns and sensibilities.

Ruth's parents shopped around for a synagogue that felt right. The one they chose was led by a rabbi Ruth's mother knew through the seminary, Milton Steinberg. He was a leading thinker, known to be wise, open, challenging of accepted practice, and controversial. In retrospect, that all of these characteristics appealed to Marjorie was no surprise to Ruth. As she has traveled the country on speaking engagements over the years, many former JTS students have approached her to share grateful memories of Marjorie. "By both their accounts and hers, she had a particular fondness for, and was most helpful to, the doubters, the rebels, and the iconoclasts." In my view, it is precisely this way of holding to tradition in a manner which is rigorously challenging, open to doubt, and even iconoclastic which marks resistance faith. Though they felt unsure of how to proceed, Ruth's parents knew they wanted some form of observance in the home as well. Marjorie's account of those first attempts, nearly sixty years old, may have striking relevance for many contemporary parents:

> We recognized that we were both religious people, but that neither of us was close to the formal observances which our society generally labels "religion." ... In our search for a technique for passing on to our children the faith and sense of security which we felt were the first values they could derive from religion, we were impressed by the importance of ritual. The difficulty for us was that we were completely unfamiliar with the ritual ourselves. We had each observed these ceremonies but they were not part of us. At the end of one long discussion we said, "Next Friday we will light candles." We felt self-conscious at the prospect of praying in public — even though our two-year-old daughter was our only public.

A while later, Marjorie was able to report:

> We are learning that rituals seem to have been designed to prompt the very questions we want our children to ask. At a special family Friday night dinner we try to answer them honestly at a child's level. ... We think our children are learning a more genuine tolerance than they could acquire any other way.

Looking back, Ruth feels her mother's relation to Judaism "dramatically defined my life." "I realized that if my mother's approach to religion, like that of so many Jews, had been to observe a little less than her parents, we would be a family committed to Jewish philanthropy and social justice but one with no religious convictions or family religious practices." She seemed to imply here that religion brings something vital and unique to the mix of the values of philanthropy and social justice, something substantive that adds rigor and strength.

In a family so thoughtful about ethical instruction, there were other topics that prompted soul-searching. At age fourteen, Ruth overheard her mother and maternal grandfather arguing over whether it was time for Ruth to know the truth about Roosevelt. Prior to this, the family had always held up Roosevelt as "a positive icon of what government was all about." But now she was hearing another view — that his administration had not done enough to intervene on behalf of the Jews. She had little context in which to place it at the time. No one in her family had been involved in the Holocaust and it was never mentioned in the household. Neither had it come up in the predominantly Protestant private school she attended.

Having grown up in the Jewishly defined world of Manhattan's Upper West Side, Ruth had never been exposed to explicit anti-Semitism. But in this East Side school, she began to get hints of being different. "And, by the way, it wasn't just Jew and non-Jew; it was also that I was one of only two Democrats in my class . . . so I got a chance to spend some time early on defining myself as sort of other."

A few years later, in her first job, she found herself the only Jew working in the foster care system in Oklahoma. Her experiences there were more unsettling. "It really was scary. It was me against the world. I was a woman; I was not a native; I was a New Yorker; I talked too fast." She described a meeting where a colleague reported a request that he find an adoptive home for a Jewish baby born out of wedlock, the only time such a request had ever occurred. The ensuing conversation indicated that everyone around the table believed that Jews did not have babies out of wedlock. Ruth spoke up and said that they did on an economic level proportional to everyone else in the country. When asked how she knew that, she disclosed that she was Jewish — a fact that no one knew or wanted to believe because the only Jew they knew had red hair and blue eyes.

Ruth felt that what she experienced there was "anti-Semitism based on ignorance, as opposed to some sort of evil intent. But I kept running into it. It was a big thing for me. I was not very old and nobody had prepared me for this." Given the strong sense of self her upbringing had given her, this experience was more eye-opening to Ruth than oppressive. Still, it was enough of a taste of the dynamics of being marginalized that she considered making sure her own children would experience something similar.

It also brought home the messages about social justice she had heard so often from her family. What Ruth and the other women leaders seemed to internalize from their own experiences was that being "other" did not — or should not — mean being less. These experiences made them acutely sensitive to those on the margins of society and served as vivid lessons in inclusiveness.

Ruth's brief tenure in the Oklahoma welfare system introduced her to local government. She felt drawn to it. Returning to New York with her young children in the mid-1960s, she knew her interests lay at the intersection of public policy and education. By 1968, parents associated with an alternative elementary school asked her to direct and represent the school, a position she held for six years. As well as sharpening her insights about the possibilities for transforming public education, her lobbying on behalf of the school brought her in touch with every elected official in the city.

It was this mix of experience and sensibilities that prompted democratic organizers in the mid-1970s to encourage Ruth to run for public office. Interestingly, this was not Ruth's parents' definition of success. Despite their convictions about civic responsibility, success for them meant choosing a known profession and rising to the top of it. Ruth had to forge her own definition of success as she took the government route.

She had help constructing it. In part, it came from some women teachers she had had along the way who were "fighting mad and challenged the excessive establishment of the school." She would also be informed by the many contacts she made while pursuing her grass-roots style of politics. Among these was a parish priest who got her involved in fighting to maintain affordable housing on the West Side. Again, it was his iconoclastic style of engagement that drew her. "He just took on the city hierarchy non-stop on issues — and he did it with deliberation and intensity. I loved him and learned a lot from him." Somewhat tongue in cheek, she told me that twenty-five hundred people risked excommunication to attend his funeral because he had fathered a family while being a priest. Her mother's daughter, she seemed to prefer religious leaders who were prepared to be "challenging and controversial."

Over the years, the Holocaust has become an important teacher as well, as her mother and grandfather knew it needed to be. For Ruth, it is a prism which reveals several key public policy issues. At the center stands the question of what people knew and when they knew it. There are educational elements arrayed around this. "What do you tell thirteen-year-olds? How do you expect them to learn about good and evil, and how do you get them the whole story?" "And this relates to the ongoing ambiguity of things — that nothing is purely one or another. This is certainly true in politics." And then there are the issues of denial or cover-up. "In a broad way, it defines how much people don't want to deal with bad news . . . which relates to what the press does and doesn't cover."

For Ruth, the power of the Holocaust prism is its ability to shed light on analogous contemporary behavior. Fascinated by the stories of Christians who protected or rescued Jews during World War II, she observes:

We can all think about what we would have done, and that's an important exercise. But it's a big remove from this more fundamental question, which is "What are you doing about poverty and inequity in the world?"

Ruth believes that it is a question of getting people the whole story about socio-political evils that still exist in our midst. All of her work in city government, and for the last decade as executive director of American Jewish World Service has been directed toward those ends.

Gathering Up the Strands

What do these women's stories reveal about the dynamics that flow together to make progressive public religious leaders? Clearly there is no simple or single recipe for concocting them. Yet it is obvious from these accounts that family models and messages are tremendously formative. When they happen in concert with a religious community, the effect is all the more powerful. If these first families, these primary spheres of influence, communicate and demonstrate that each of us has a role to play in repairing the brokenness of our world, doing so becomes second nature. It is then not so much an act of courage as it is a loyalty to a conviction of how the world is. One knows this because one has lived it within a small community — a family at least; a family, a village, and a religious community at best. With any luck, it grows outward from there.

We are not talking about idyllic childhoods, at least not in the usual sense of the word. We are talking about learning that suffering and oppression are part of the way the world now is (maybe even how our own family is), but that addressing it with a sense of meaning and efficacy is also who we are. We are talking about having early experiences of "right relationship" which develop our own moral compass and which prepare us for the necessity of questioning conventional wisdom. We do so not for the sake of acting out, but because we have seen that a more complete justice comes of it. Because we have lived with people doing it, we have learned never to stop closing the gap between this world and a better one. When we wonder how to do this, adults recognize us for the gifts we now have, and contributions we may one day make. Graced by inclusiveness lessons of all kinds, we are increasingly prepared to think of every human as potential kin. Stung by the betrayals and shortcomings of our religious traditions, we find we can still tap a deeper vein of blessing and guidance. We resolve that religion, too, has a gap between what it is and what it could be, and that we want to play a role in that evolution. It gradually dawns on us that we are here, in the company of others, in the shadow of millennia, to be part of an ongoing transformation toward wholeness. It feels like something we can't not do.

If this is the stuff of our youth and young adulthood, then precisely because of the way the gaps and suffering have been seen, acknowledged, held, and countered, it will have been idyllic indeed — idyllic in its root sense of wise vision.

In the end we all have to gather up the strands of our lives and try to make something worthy of them — to fashion whole cloth out of the bits and pieces. Examining these women's lives led me on a journey of my own. I was tremendously moved by their courage, often in the face of great odds. I guarantee their stories will work on you, the reader, too. In the next chapter we will consider how that might happen as we look more closely at how their lives prompted me to found Face to Face/Faith to Faith. We shall also consider how certain progressive religious leadership capacities can be nurtured, especially in educational settings like seminaries and rabbinical schools. Finally, we'll look specifically at the qualities and capacities that many religious leaders need in an increasingly complex, pluralistic society.

Chapter 9

TAKING THE LEAP

Sometimes your vocation discovers you when you least expect it. If you are reading this book, chances are that something like what happened to me may be happening in you. In the summer of 2000, Iliff School of Theology in Denver invited me to teach a course about the patterns of leadership I was noticing in the women whose work I had been following. I called it *The Public Leadership of Women of Faith*. Since I wanted my class to have the experience of actually doing interviews with progressive, faith-motivated women doing groundbreaking work, I asked Dr. Pamela Eisenbaum, my friend and colleague at Iliff, to help me find some candidates in the area. This is how I met Melodye Feldman, founder of Seeking Common Ground, an organization focused on grassroots peacebuilding. We were fortunate to spend a few hours with her because summer is the high season for one of her core programs, Building Bridges for Peace. Camped amid the dramatic and peaceful Colorado mountains, Israeli, Palestinian, and American young women spend several consuming weeks trying to unravel the charged emotions and enduring conflicts that haunt their relationships and everyday lives.

My students were captivated by Melodye's account of how her current work is rooted in her own history. She told us how one afternoon as she walked home from school in Miami, Florida, some of her junior high school peers had physically attacked her and taunted her for being Jewish. Melodye felt instinctively that if these kids had known her, they would have liked her. The next day she went to the principal's office and asked for her help in putting together a forum where kids could explore each other's differences, talk about stereotypes, and get to know one another better.

She helped Melodye put these educational goals into practice, and she was off and running. The seeds of working to build bridges across lines of difference were planted. Melodye's religious journey took her from roots in the Conservative movement to an Orthodox Yeshiva as a teenager to her current affiliation as a Reconstructionist Jew. Her professional career includes many years of Jewish camping, a Social Work degree, work in the field of domestic violence (including with perpetrators), and a private therapy practice.

In the early 1990s, Melodye chanced to hear a radio show that changed her life. A teenage girl in the war-torn region of the former Yugoslavia was being interviewed by a journalist over the din of gunfire. Even the park where they met had been devastated by warfare, its gracious wooden benches long gone for firewood. This young girl expressed no interest in living, despite her upcoming birthday, because her future offered so little hope. Melodye remembered the promise of her own life at sixteen and vowed on the spot to dedicate the rest of her life to teaching young leaders to build bridges of peace and understanding in the communities where they lived.

When I met Melodye that summer, I had been a Presbyterian minister for almost twenty years and part of building Auburn Seminary for almost a decade, focusing on fundraising, administration, and building new program initiatives, especially in the multifaith arena. But the stories of the women leaders I had been tracking were working their alchemy in me. So, too, were the troubling findings highlighted in Auburn's research report, *Missing Connections,* about the invisibility of religious leaders in the public arena. As creative as my Auburn work was, I realized that something was missing. I wanted to do more to demonstrate possibilities for public leadership.

The Story of Face to Face/Faith to Faith

As my Denver class finished its interview with Melodye, I heard myself spontaneously asking her whether she ever came to New York. "Yes," she said, and within three months she and I were sitting in my office at Auburn dreaming up Face to Face/Faith to Faith. Years earlier the Auburn board had envisioned that some of Auburn's multifaith work should be focused on young leaders, but for me the catalytic moment came with our meeting.

Dreaming an Idea into Being: The Power of Partnerships

The framework took shape almost immediately: an international youth leadership program with young men and women, weaving together strengths from each of our current organizations. Seeking Common Ground brought expertise in peacemaking, communication methodologies, and working with teenagers from conflict areas. Auburn offered its experience with multifaith education and a broad network of contacts in a variety of religious communities. Melodye came as a therapist, peace educator, and activist, and I brought my training as a minister, educator, and administrator.

Face to Face/Faith to Faith's mission would be to educate tomorrow's leaders as peacemakers and faith-based activists in places of conflict around the world. We hoped to plant the kinds of seeds that would grow leaders like the women in this book. One of our guiding questions became: How can our religious traditions, so often used to wage war, be resources for making peace? We decided to include young men and women because the real world in which peacemaking must happen includes both. They would come from conflict zones all around the world — Israel and Palestine, South Africa, Northern Ireland, and the United States — and would be Jews, Christians, Muslims, and Hindus. We felt that the participants' exposure to one another needed to do

more than facilitate positive feelings and promote dialogue. It needed
to sponsor action and the ongoing practice of activism. We wanted to
help these young people find partners in the work and common cause
to heal and repair the world.

In choosing the program title, we drew upon the story in the book
of Genesis about Jacob and Esau, twin brothers estranged for many
years by acts of betrayal and rage, who find a way to avert war and
dwell together again in a shared homeland. At the moment of reunion,
Jacob says to his brother, "to see your face is like seeing the face of
God." This is our hope for the program — that fears of annihilation
will be replaced by joy over enduring kinship, that wrestling with the
demons and angels in our midst may grant us surprising blessings.

Audacity requires funding. Our inspiration, arising from the work
of both Auburn and Seeking Common Ground, found close and ready
partners in Auburn board member Mark Hostetter and his partner
Alex Habib. With seed money in hand, Melodye and I simply began.
At every step, I heard the voices of the women leaders in this book
whispering encouragement. Their practices began to feel familiar as
Melodye and I worked out our own story of women's collaborative
leadership. Now in its fifth year, Face to Face has become flesh on the
bones of theory this book outlines.

Face to Face/Faith to Faith Today

For several weeks every summer a new Face to Face community of
eighty or so persons gathers at a conference center an hour north
of New York City: new students, ages sixteen to eighteen; a cohort
of returning student leaders in training, counselors, and leaders; and
an assortment of other specialists — religious leaders, activists, artists,
slam poets, musicians. We are a dense mix of traditions: Protestants
and Catholics from Belfast, evangelical Christians from South Africa,
Palestinian Christians, members of U.S. mainline churches. There are
Orthodox Jews from Israel, a Jew from Northern Ireland (one of the

few), members of the vibrant Orthodox community in Cape Town, and Reform and Conservative Jews from the United States. Muslims come from around the world, including young women who cover and those who do not, and those who experience and practice Islam in a multiplicity of ways. Many of our students have known other religious groups only as a hated enemy and have been admonished before coming "don't speak to those Jews . . . those Catholics . . . those Muslims." Many have never met "the other" before.

Communication in a Holding Environment

Like the women leaders in this book, we create a holding environment, a space set apart from the students' home communities, with enough security to allow students to let down their usual defenses, yet enough challenge to prod them to take risks to become human beings and relate authentically to one another. The curriculum is focused on developing the communication skills necessary for navigating difficult, charged conversations. An Israeli student may share with Palestinians the loss of friends in a bombing. A Palestinian may share the degradation and humiliation at the hands of Israeli soldiers at checkpoints. A child of Manhattan may explore the guilt and responsibility of living with enormous privilege in the United States. Another may talk of the schizophrenia of being an American Muslim post-9/11, trying simultaneously to fit into school and culture while meeting the expectations of a traditional home life and religious mandates. Many of our students have experienced the loss of friends, parents, and members of their communities from violence. Instead of theirs being the only valid perspective, they begin to hear the multiple perspectives and narratives that shape the human story. The "prisms of pain"[40] that have locked them into a narrow view of reality give way as other perspectives seep in. The story of "me" and "my people" takes its place among other narratives, reshaping itself into the larger narrative of "we" and "us."

Students explore their identities as individuals, parts of families and communities, the wider human community, and the global reality.

Multifaith Education

Exploring religious identity is a major part of the curriculum. Participants learn about each other's religious traditions in an atmosphere of inquiry, openness, and sensitivity. This form of multifaith education involves neither syncretism (blending elements of different faith, rituals, or practices of worship) nor selective instruction (focusing only on the attractive or convenient elements of various traditions while omitting others). Further, while some people are afraid that exposure to other traditions will erode a person's faith or tempt them to convert to another, anyone involved in multifaith education knows the opposite is true. If anything, people become more curious about their own faith and are carried to a deeper understanding of it. There is nothing like having to explain one's faith to someone from a different tradition that forces one to clarify what one believes.

During the program, students begin to map their own experiences of religion. Who taught them? What were the messages? How does religion feature in the conflicts that they experience in their communities and countries? How are religion, politics, and culture interconnected? What do our traditions and texts tell us about gender and class? Who claims religious authority? We often look at difficult sacred texts from our traditions, the ones that seem to justify war and violence. We all have them. What do those texts teach about the stranger? We look too at our sacred texts which tell a different story about reaching out to the stranger, about hospitality, and about being peacemakers. Students begin to see that the story is more complex than they had thought.

We have religious leaders on hand to respond to "any question you ever had" about another religious tradition. A Catholic priest, in the wake of pedophilia scandals, is grilled about celibacy, women's ordination, or his personal experience of call to the priesthood.

A rabbi is pressed about Zionism, the building of the Separation Barrier/wall/fence in Israel, and the laws of Kashrut.

In one exercise, students are invited to place themselves on a continuum in response to theological questions. "Place yourself on the left side of the room if you believe that one day all people will live in peace, on the other side if you believe that there will always be war and violence, or place yourself somewhere in between," says the leader. Students move across the room, literally taking a stand for their position. Then there is opportunity for discussion about why they stand where they do, and the opportunity to change their minds and move to another spot on the continuum. Then another question: "Does prayer matter?" Yes to one side, no to the other, and so on. Amidst all the backs and forths, students come face to face with people from other traditions with whom they may have more in common than they do with someone in another wing of their own tradition. Appreciation grows for the great variety of religious perspectives. Students begin to claim their own authority as they become interpreters of their own traditions.

Activism/Service Learning

Along with communication and multifaith awareness, the program sponsors an informed activism. Paul Knitter, a passionate advocate of interreligious cooperation, has influenced us greatly. Key to cooperation, he feels, is keeping the largest possible context in view. Knitter predicts that by assuming responsibility for alleviating crises afflicting the entire globe — such as war, poverty, and ecological degradation — religionists will make two kinds of progress at once. "With global responsibility as the arena for interfaith discourse," Knitter argues, "... the religions will not only be able to contribute to resolving our global crises, but they will also be able to understand, learn from and enhance each other as never before."[41] Face to Face emphasizes the imperative for peaceful co-existence that lies at the core of our religious traditions.

To this end, Face to Face students are exposed to adult activists whose work to change the world is faith motivated. One is Ruth Messinger, whose story we heard earlier in this book. Or Julio Medina, formerly incarcerated for life, who, upon release from prison, became a Christian minister and founded Exodus Transition Community in order to help ex-prisoners negotiate a return to life on the "outside." Or Farid Esack, a Muslim, and former minister for gender equality in the New South Africa, who, as a scholar/activist, is developing a more progressive understanding of Islam. Students hear Farid's story of his relationship to the other, formed by his childhood neighbor, Mrs. Beddis, a Catholic woman across the back fence, who shared her food with him and his hungry siblings, and shared her friendship with Farid's mother, the single parent of many boys. When Farid was sent to study in a maddrassah in Pakistan, he could not reconcile the strict Islam he was being taught — including the tenet that non-Muslims would not go to heaven — with his experience of this good Catholic neighbor who had saved their very lives. If heaven existed, she would surely be there too, he thought.

Engaged by these adult examples of seamless lives, students gain momentum for putting their own deepest convictions into practice. Before coming to the summer intensive, our students have already committed themselves to work with Face to Face at home for at least one year. During the summer intensive, students meet with their home groups, facilitated by an adult staff member from their home country, to plan the projects of service learning and activism they will pursue after returning home. This may mean gathering parents and families to share what they have learned from the Face to Face intensive; making presentations and holding workshops in their schools or religious communities; working on the HIV/AIDS crisis in South Africa;

developing cross-community relationships in Northern Ireland; contributing to a conference on the divisions of race, culture, and class in Denver; or working toward new possibilities for peace in Israel.

All students must do written work, demonstrate learning, and experiment with activism before graduating from Face to Face. The main message we hope to convey to them is that they have agency and a unique role to play in changing the world, that they are inextricably bound in a global web of connection.

Letting Go and Passing It On

Just as the lives of the women leaders in this book have worked to encourage me, Melodye and I know we have been powerful symbols for the students in our program. We are unabashed feminists with progressive values, each of us rooted in her religious tradition, trying to model the messages we preach. Yet given our goal of cultivating young leaders, as well as the recognition that as we both turn fifty we may no longer be the best ones to work directly with teenagers, we find ourselves in transition.

At this stage in the program, many of our staff are former program participants, some of whom we have been educating, mentoring, and nurturing for over five years. Their choices for education, career, and vocation have been dramatically influenced by their extended exposure to Face to Face/Faith to Faith. It seems right that they now take on more of the responsibility for the one-on-one leadership. Melodye and I plan to expand our own work on the systemic dimensions of peacemaking. Yet aware as we are of the dynamism of the one-on-one systemic dance (described in chapter 3), we will continue to stay well connected to the program.

In thinking about this transition, the practice of Buddhist sand painting comes to my mind. Monks lavish days of attention on the fashioning of a large, intricately colored mandala. At its completion, they simply sweep it away, illustrating their lack of attachment to it and the impermanence of all things. The message is that even things of great beauty — the products of energy, imagination, and love — are not static and permanent but constantly changing. Unlike the sand painting, Face to Face will endure, but it will surely evolve as new leaders join us with fresh ideas and as Melodye and I learn to fold our wider peacemaking efforts back into the program's design.

Finding and Retaining the Right Partners

It would be remiss of me not to attempt full disclosure about the work of building such a program and the nature of this partnership between Melodye and me. As wonderful as women's collaborations can be, it is important to recognize that they can also be painful, as challenging as marriage or life partnership, or more so. Sometimes feminists mask these difficulties, intent as they are on celebrating collaboration and sisterhood. I must say that Melodye and I have learned that peacemaking is an ongoing discipline at the micro level as well as the macro.

Our differences that so often combine into strength can also be our greatest challenge. Melodye is the founder of a grassroots organization, comes from a psychology and social work background, and has often worked almost exclusively in the company of young staff. This can be both energizing and lonely. Melodye's interest in religion focuses on its role in waging war and making peace. I come from the world of academia and Auburn, an almost two-hundred-year-old institution, which is stable but lean. I am a clergy person who is often at odds with my denomination, but basically sees value and possibility in organized religion. Between us there are two organizations, two boards, one thousand miles, and ongoing programs on several continents — considerable logistical and administrative challenges. But forging a partnership has also meant creating shared space that can hold and acknowledge two strong-willed people, both with deep convictions and high control needs. Trust has been tentative at times and hard won. Periodically, we turn to the expert coaching of a friend and supporter of the program, Barbara Moss, whom we both trust. She has helped us to see not only the enemy or stranger in this sister-other, but the face of God. The reality is that the two of us dedicated to peace have had to work so hard to create a holding environment for ourselves. Peacemaking at all levels is an ongoing process of engagement with each other. Yet as the stories of so many biblical characters attest, God can use us, imperfect as we are, to create programs as promising as Face to Face/Faith to Faith.

A second dimension of partnership is the ongoing task of securing funding. Although the women leaders I interviewed did not dwell on finances and fundraising, the onus of it was a subtext running throughout the interviews. Connie Baugh even extracted a promise from me: "Do not forget to talk about money." The truth is, raising money is both heartening and extremely frustrating. We were able to launch Face to Face quickly because we had supportive and eager funders who knew just the right balance of staying involved and committed, yet giving us the space to move forward with the guidance and oversight of our boards. Since the initial launch, we have added other generous friends, who work tirelessly to raise about one half million dollars a year for this program. More daunting is achieving sustainability so that we can keep the current program running while planning for expansion like adding sessions or countries and working more extensively with systems, including parents, religious communities, and schools.

It is a question of creating and sustaining the conviction in others that the work is worthy, that it contributes real value to our world, that to invest in it will make a meaningful difference. Without these kinds of alliances, the work cannot go forward. When someone asks us about the expense of Face to Face, we often point out the comparative billions of dollars it takes to wage war in Iraq for example, or to rebuild the post-war infrastructure in Afghanistan, or launch a global war on terror. Melodye often offers that surely there is money enough to support peace programs powerful enough to compete with terrorist training camps. What is the cost of failing to provide an alternative means of engaging the imagination and idealism of our teenagers and young adults?

We need partners of all kinds to do the work. We are heartened, strengthened, and made more effective when we find them. But it takes ongoing work to tend them, adjust and prune as necessary, and ensure that the whole mix of influences they represent contributes to the type of holding environment one's organization needs in order to endure.

A Palette of Competencies

Listening to the voices of the women leaders in this book and finding their insights born out in my own experience with Face to Face brings clearer focus to the question of what competencies are required of a religious leader in a pluralist context. Since the cultivation of such leadership is central to Auburn Seminary's mission, I often think about how a seminary can best help people develop these capacities. The broad answer, it seems to me now, is by helping them *make connections.* This is deceptively simple to say, but more difficult to practice with potentially world-changing integrity. Yet it may well be the most potent antidote to the haunting situation identified in Auburn's research study, *Missing Connections.* If we hope to educate religious leaders who will be visible, viable resources in our most important deliberations and policy initiatives, we need to help them build competencies of connection — to people of other religious traditions, to the living core of their own symbols, between their deepest convictions and their professional choices, and to the ethical dimensions of public issues.

I see better now that Auburn is already doing much of this work, though we are adding, testing, and tuning programs all the time. I think of Auburn as a holding environment of sorts, a laboratory where ideas about and education for leadership are both incubated and implemented, where people are given space to address pressing controversial issues and are challenged to grow in new ways through engagement with themselves, with others, and with the Divine. Auburn is a mediating institution, with one foot in the world of academia and the other in local religious communities of leaders and seekers alike.

"Hardiness" is a word that animated Auburn's founders almost two hundred years ago. Back then it was meant to describe ministers tough enough for life on the geographical frontier and grounded enough to communicate the gospel in a warm-hearted, accessible way. It remains for us an evocative word. As we think about preparing religious leaders — be they pulpit clergy, lay people, or faith-based public leaders like the women in this book — what will make them hardy? What specific competencies will help them take root and thrive in modern contexts? Based on our experiences here at Auburn, and informed by the accounts of the women leaders in this book, I would suggest that competencies in four broad areas need to be supported:

- Multifaith literacy and a conversion to pluralism
- Public issue literacy and media savvy
- Tapping networks of support
- Living a feminist ethic of connection

Multifaith Literacy and Conversion to Pluralism

I believe that how our religions *relate to each other* is the most important issue for the future. Yet it is still possible to become an ordained clergy person — a rabbi, minister, priest, or imam — without becoming deeply conversant with other religious traditions. Lay leaders are vulnerable to this as well. To be sure, curricula and requirements are already seemingly stretched to capacity just trying to develop familiarity with the texts, theology, and history of a single tradition. Nevertheless, it is essential that we support religious leaders of all kinds — emerging ones and those long in practice — in developing an awareness of other traditions. A single comparative religion survey course will not suffice. The capacity needed is a knowledge of other religions as living traditions with rituals, observances, theologies and beliefs, histories and practices. Religionists must become more adept at viewing their own and other traditions not as monolithic entities, but rather as varied distillations of a host of subtleties and distinctions. Cultivating this deeper awareness involves the risk of authentic engagement with others — not only mediated through books, the Internet, and classroom lectures, but up close through observing worship and prayer, sharing meals and rituals of celebration, studying sacred texts, and understanding how people read and interpret such texts differently.

Interwoven with such explorations there quite naturally arises a deeper inspection of the symbols and tenets of one's own tradition. This becomes an opportunity to make the kinds of discoveries the women in this book made as they labored to convey the core teachings of their own traditions to others. Diving deeper, they pressed beyond the formulaic insider language and touched anew the radical roots. It is these freshly unearthed meanings, appreciated in light of dialogue with other traditions, which hold such potential for building the language bridges we need for collaborative efforts.

In multifaith education, then, the movement is simultaneously outward and inward, horizontal and vertical, farther afield and closer to home. Paradoxically, it carries us to a place where self and other are felt to be both more distinct and more truly linked. It cultivates the ability to recognize and honor what Rabbi Jonathan Sacks has termed "the dignity of difference." The more we can do this, he says, the more of God will be revealed.

We encounter God in the face of a stranger. That, I believe, is the Hebrew Bible's single greatest and most counterintuitive contribution to ethics. God creates difference; therefore it is in one-who-is-different that we meet God.... The human other is a trace of the Divine Other.... The supreme religious challenge is to see God's image in one who is not in our image. That is the converse of tribalism. But it is also something other than universalism. It takes difference seriously.... The critical test of any order is: does it make space for otherness? Does it acknowledge the dignity of difference?[42]

Taking difference seriously brings about what I call a conversion to pluralism — a critical counterbalance to dangerous tribalism. Wilfred Cantwell Smith, late scholar of world religions, says this involves taking both a broader view and a firmer hold. "The issue of pluralism," he writes, "is... how to enlarge one's vision of truth without losing loyalty to one's own, however finite, hold upon it (by it)."[43] Being converted to pluralism means keeping our attention focused on that which is larger than any one of us, on the broadest possible context for our actions. This, ironically, makes each particular foothold on the planet smaller yet more weighty. Each of us learns that we play a vital part in a revelation none can accomplish alone. As Smith puts it,

What is beginning to happen around the earth today is the incredibly exciting development that will eventually mean that each person, certainly each group, participates in the religious history of humankind — as self-consciously the context for faith.

I do not mean that Christians will cease to be Christians, or Muslims Muslim. What I mean is that Christians will participate, as Christians, in the religious history of humankind; Muslims will participate in it as Muslims, Jews as Jews, Hindus as Hindus, Buddhists as Buddhists.[44]

I believe that God chooses to reveal God's Self in many ways. It makes me no less a Christian to whom God has been most clearly revealed in Jesus Christ to learn from, be curious about, and come to respect the Jew, the Muslim, the Jain, or Buddhist. Can we really afford to think otherwise? As Sacks counsels, "We will make peace only when we learn that God loves difference, and so, at last must we. God has created many cultures, civilizations and faiths but only one world in which to live together — and it is getting smaller all the time."[45]

If we can make the leap of converting to pluralism and cast our attention where it belongs — on the one precious and finite world we share — then so much else becomes possible. If we help religious leaders develop a theology of difference, we create the foundation for working together with others in concert with God to change and redeem the world.

Public Issue Literacy and Media Savvy

As the women leaders I interviewed emphasized, central to all religions is the charge to do justice, love kindness, care for the disenfranchised, and repair the world. Going public with religious leadership is simply integral to the call. Silence is not an option, and preoccupation with institutional maintenance is insufficient. We need programs which help leaders do their homework in this area, programs that develop public issue literacy. The stories of the women in this book represent some key social issues: human rights, criminal justice system reform, immigration reform, care for children, the elderly, the disabled, the battered. But we also need leaders who can unravel and speak to the ethical issues embedded in such areas as bioengineering, environmental threats, medical technologies, business outsourcing, and historical conflicts around the world.

This does not mean that every minister or rabbi or lay leader must become expert in every public issue, but it does mean exploring one or two in enough depth to appreciate its complexities, specialized language, key players, and historical development. My issue, for instance, is the Israeli-Palestinian conflict. Though I am far from an expert, I am an avid learner about its relationship historically and theologically to my Presbyterian denomination and how it features in the broader unfolding drama in the Middle East and around the world. I pursue this by getting to know the Face to Face teenagers, visiting the region to learn about the quality of life for Palestinians and Israelis, convening tables of conversation about the issue at Auburn, and reading and hearing from experts. It also means inviting myself to tables where religious leaders do not normally get invited!

Churches and synagogues and mosques need to send and support the message that public issues like these are intimately and inextricably related to the faith. They should build in time for their leaders to do public issue homework and to preach about it from the pulpit. No one should graduate from seminary or rabbinical school — or, I would suggest, become a lay leader in a local congregation — without having developed some understanding of their identity as a public leader and a beginning passion for and competency in at least one public issue. Remember that a number of the leaders in this book identified field work — where they received a hands-on experience of people in need and the beginnings of a systemic perspective on the problem — as the single most important element of their formal training. This finding should give seminary educators pause as they assign value to the various aspects of their students' formation and preparation. Field education, supported by relevant theory and discussion, needs to be viewed as central to the learning experience.

Developing oneself as a public leader means not only having public issue literacy but actually going public with it and being savvy about how to do so. Auburn identified several years ago that we hear only a narrow band of religious leaders on radio and television, and that the public imagination would be better served by hearing thoughtful spokespersons from all across the spectrum. We feel religious leaders need to take their place among economists, politicians, lawyers, educators, and scientists who are asked to comment on the day's developments. In response, we have created Auburn Media, a multi-pronged program which (1) helps religionists develop media expertise, (2) introduces and markets to the media the most articulate religious voices, and (3) sponsors or produces educational programs using the best media, such as documentary film, on religion and ethics. With Auburn Media we are trying to create invitations to the "table" of public discourse that do not currently exist for religious leaders.

As the stories of the women in this book show, being articulate in our pluralist/secular society means being able to translate insights for a variety of audiences and being sensitive to context. Our seminaries and rabbinical schools already help students learn to address their own communities of faith in compelling ways within the idiom of each community. But going public with faith-based leadership calls for even more consciousness about language. We need to devise programs and convene discussions which help leaders discover and use the most effective language for speaking to a broader public, many of whom come from other religious traditions or who are avowed secularists. Some of this capacity will arise naturally as a by-product of multi-faith education, but the ability to translate across domains is such a key means of making connections that it deserves attention as a topic unto itself.

Tapping Networks of Support

While the women leaders I interviewed spoke of the remarkably deep and abiding satisfaction they took from their work, they also noted significant costs — lack of family or personal time, financial pressures, loss of privacy, and loss of innocence from exposure to human tragedy and violence. Through focused work at Auburn with Christian clergy, we are aware of these and other stressors inherent in ministry and other religious vocations: diffuse goals and multiple demands, insufficient time for continued study and learning, low salaries, decreasing professional status in the culture, and isolation. From 2003 through 2005,

Auburn Seminary, in partnership with Union and New York Theological Seminaries and with the support of Lilly Endowment, offered a Sabbatical Institute for sixty Christian clergy during which various supportive strategies were piloted and evaluated. A key finding of this program was that helping these leaders *make connections* was one of the most effective antidotes to stress and burnout.

At the Institute, participants found two forms of personal connection particularly restorative: peer relationships and professional coaching. Remember how much Laura Jervis appreciated her "cabal" of women friends and colleagues? She considered this small group of peers her lifeline, the ones who helped her to take heart and be bold when she faltered, or to strategize about how to approach key issues. Because of their unique role as the keepers of confidences, ministers often cannot be fully candid with members of their own community, and the demands of the work may dissuade them from investing in a cabal of their own. My own research and the findings of the Institute suggest that it is essential that religious leaders be supported in carving out the time necessary to sustain these peer relationships.

Executive coaching is an intervention that has been used effectively in the corporate world for some time, but it is quite new for the religious world and its leaders. I was a skeptic myself until I tried it with a coach whose clients were mostly corporate executives and celebrities. It has been the single most valuable strategy that has helped me grow. Based on our experiences in the Sabbatical Institute, we feel that a coaching relationship can also be an essential connection for religious leaders as they negotiate the complex challenges facing them. A coach is an advocate who offers perspective and clarity from outside the system in which a leader works, although at times it can be fruitful for the coach to witness a person in their professional settings — chairing meetings, leading worship, or making a speech, for instance. Unlike therapy, coaching is strategic, short-term, and action-oriented, designed to identify professional and personal goals as well as specific steps for reaching them. As a second set of eyes and ears, a coach can help a leader develop more consciousness about dynamics that block progress or strengths that may have gone uncelebrated. Taking a step back and working candidly with a coach, a leader in danger of burnout may be able to identify trauma triggers and ways to work through them, rearticulate a sense of calling, or gain clarity on how to make major transitions. Responses to our pilot program suggest that coaching can help leaders feel more confident and successful in their work, less isolated, and enjoy a greater sense of agency about the work ahead.

In addition to peer relationships and coaching, there is a third type of support network which is essential for sustaining the work: developing alliances with funders. Fundraising is a skill that anyone who wants to change the world must eventually develop, especially if they seek to create new programs and approaches like the women I interviewed did. Many of them learned the art by doing it, as I have done. What I have come to understand is that, at its core, fundraising is about developing a genuine relationship with people who happen to have financial resources to share. If you really believe in a cause, you will find a way to convey that vision and enthusiasm in an infectious way. People want to make a difference in whatever ways they can. Consider that your project gives them that opportunity. Each party to the partnership, then, is both giver and receiver, and a gratifying sense of shared enterprise grows. Over the years, I have developed true friendships with donors in which we share our personal and professional sorrows, joys, and successes. It also helps to become a "philanthropist" oneself, whatever one's capacity is. Notice whatever feelings of resistance, fear, and joy come when you give your own money away. Then you will understand what others may feel when you ask them to invest in your work.

The challenge of funding projects like Face to Face becomes easier as a growing number of enlightened women philanthropists recognize the power of well-chosen investments. It is important to note that women control 51 percent of the wealth of this country,[46] so their capacity to use money strategically to change the world is enormous. These are not necessarily women of enormous wealth. There are a growing number of women's funding networks and foundations that are helping women at all economic levels to use their resources to put their convictions and passions behind grassroots ventures.

Women donors (and men too!) are becoming more informed all the time, realizing that one year of funding may not be enough, that a small organization may need to gain a diversified funding portfolio before being weaned from original sources. This takes time and patience on the part of funders. Enlightened organizations like The New York Women's Foundation even offer add-on value beyond grant dollars to grantees. They help grassroots organizations which are focused on low-income women and girls build their infrastructures and capacity through technical assistance on management and leadership, non-profit administration, and fundraising itself.

Living a Feminist Ethic of Connection

Finally, if we follow the example of the women leaders in this book, we will come to understand that all of these competencies flow from an overarching conviction about how interconnected and interdependent life is. Viewed from this perspective, the task is not so much one of adding specific competencies to one's repertoire. The primary challenge which beckons us here is actually living as if everything is connected. It seems to me that doing so is what carried the women I interviewed into their seamless lives. They dared to practice, or could not help but incarnate, a feminist ethic of connection.

Though they did not dwell in the interviews on the feminist movement per se, all of them came of age at a time when it was new and potent. Many of their sensibilities about repairing the brokenness of our world derive from feminist insights about inclusiveness, relationship, process, and context. These form the bedrock of their commitments, and mine as well. While I know that the feminism that awakened and quickened me does not necessarily resonate with my children, and that feminism itself can be handled as an exclusivist ideology, I believe these women help us see feminist ethics at their best. For me, learning to fully live a feminist ethic of connection remains a compelling path toward the possibility of justice and healing for all people.

Equipping the Saints

This phrase, "equipping the saints," from the apostle Paul, evokes for me of what I hope this book can mean for readers of all kinds. I hope it will fortify, equip, and inspire you for your role in healing the world. Whether you claim the title "religious leader" or consider yourself "spiritual, but not religious," whether you are a man or a woman, I hope that the lives of the leaders in this book will inspire you to discover or reconnect with your deepest passions for making a difference. Dare to dream them forward. Act audaciously in their behalf. Remember that the women leaders in this book often knew nothing about the public issues that caught their attention. It was opening their hearts to human need and risking a response that was the catalyst. Opting out is not viable, for God can use all of us, however incapable we may feel. The women in this book have acted as a palimpsest for my own life, the layers and threads of their stories calling to my own in a way that brought more of me into being. Perhaps a bit of this alchemy will have its way with you too.

Not everyone who reads this book will found an organization — some will be volunteers and others, funders — but I hope that veterans and beginners alike will find support here for the work of repairing our world. I know that these leaders' stories can help reframe career or vocational issues at any age. Barbara Moss, friend and Auburn board member, who has achieved every success in the corporate world, recently began to yearn for something more. Now in her late fifties, she is finding new meaning by deploying her considerable skills, energy, and money on Face to Face and environmental causes. She has moved from being a careful, modest contributor to acting as a bold, strategic, and generous philanthropist. She has downsized to a more modest living space, realizing that giving away money and engaging in these meaningful non-profit pursuits is more satisfying than all the *things* money could buy. What we work *for* really does matter, and the more it is in alignment with our deepest beliefs, the more whole we become. As she closes in on her sixth decade, my friend has discovered the secret of a seamless life!

I have written this book to honor women around the world who are pursuing their own special calling to heal the world. Some have asked me why men were not among the leaders I interviewed. My answer is simple. In twenty years of ministry, when I scanned the horizon for people doing the work of progressive faith-based leadership, women were most in evidence. There are men doing this work to be sure, but fundamentally it is women who are there at the grassroots level making the difference. It is time for us to see and celebrate that. We have reached an important cusp. Momentum is gathering.

Yet so many more of us, men and women, will need to learn and live this ethic of connection if we are to be whole and at peace. I hope that as you go about your work in the world you will begin to recognize the attributes of these leaders' lives mirrored in your own and that you will take heart:

- a belief that people and systems can be transformed, appearances to the contrary;

- an entrepreneurial spirit and the conviction that one person really can make a difference;

- a counterintuitive move to embrace pain and suffering in order to redeem it;

- a belief in inclusiveness because everyone is made in God's image and God's face is most clearly seen in the one who is different from us;

- a faith that resists the status quo and embodies the radical messages of justice and love at the heart of all our religious traditions;

- the humility to consider the validity of religious traditions other than our own;

- a willingness to speak out and not keep silent;

- the commitment to find the public issues that you most care about and become expert in them;

- the urge to bring your actions and your deepest convictions into alignment, pressing toward a seamless life.

If you feel your soul wanting to respond, trust it. Act. Be one of those who does not turn away. So much is at stake.

NOTES

Chapter 1: Silence Is an Act

1. Elizabeth Lynn and Barbara G. Wheeler, *Missing Connections: Public Perceptions of Theological Education and Religious Leadership,* Auburn Studies 6 (New York: Auburn Theological Seminary, 1999). See also Diana L. Eck, *A New Religious America: How a "Christian Country" Has Become the World's Most Religiously Diverse Nation* (San Francisco: HarperSanFrancisco, 2002).

2. Stephen L. Carter, *The Culture of Disbelief: How American Law and Politics Trivialize Religious Devotion* (New York: Doubleday Anchor Books, 1993).

3. Lynn and Wheeler, *Missing Connections.*

4. Sweet Honey in the Rock, *Selections 1976–1988,* "Ella's Song," music and lyrics by Bernice Johnson Reagon (Songtalk Publishing Co., BMI, 1982).

5. Association to Benefit Children, Annual Report. See *www.a-b-c.org.*

Chapter 2: The Treasure in the Dark

6. Peter McManus et al., "Recent Trends in the Use of Antidepressant Drugs in Australia, 1990–1998," *Medical Journal of Australia* 173 (November 2000): 458–61. Published on the Internet at *www.mja.com.au/public/issues.*

7. Shankar Vedantam, "Antidepressant Use in Children Soars Despite Efficacy Doubts," *Washington Post,* April 18, 2004, A01.

8. Edward F. Edinger, *Anatomy of the Psyche* (La Salle, IL: Open Court, 1985), 9.

9. Ibid., 12.

10. Ibid., 5.

11. Donald Winnicott, *The Maturational Process* (New York: International University Press, 1965).

12. Ronald A. Heifetz, *Leadership without Easy Answers* (Cambridge, MA: The Belknap Press of Harvard University Press, 1994), 104–5.

13. Won-Jae Hur, "The Cross at Her Feet: The Ministry and Theological Voice of Korean Women at the Rainbow Center," unpublished manuscript, May 1997, 20.

14. Judith Herman, *Trauma and Recovery* (New York: HarperCollins, 1992).

15. Mindy Fullilove, *The House of Joshua: Meditations on Family and Place* (Lincoln: University of Nebraska Press, 1999), 6.

16. Frederick Buechner, *Wishful Thinking: A Theological ABC* (New York: Harper & Row, 1973), 95.

Chapter 3: Every Person Is a Universe

17. See *spend-* in "Indo-European Roots," *The American Heritage Dictionary of the English Language,* ed. William Morris (Boston and New York: American Heritage Publishing Co. and Houghton Mifflin Co., 1970).

18. Sally Helgesen, *The Web of Inclusion* (New York: Currency Doubleday, 1995), 12–13.

Chapter 4: Leading from Behind, Within, and Beneath

19. For more on the artist mode as it relates to leadership see Sharon Daloz Parks, *Leadership Can Be Taught: A Bold Approach for a Complex World* (Boston: Harvard Business School Press, 2005).

20. C. G. Jung, *Memories, Dreams, Reflections* (New York: Pantheon Books, 1973), 325.

21. Heifetz, *Leadership without Easy Answers,* and Sally Helgesen, *The Female Advantage* (New York: Currency Doubleday, 1990). For a discussion of the movement toward a more adequate myth of leadership, see Parks, *Leadership Can Be Taught,* chapter 9.

22. See *per-5* in "Indo-European Roots," *The American Heritage Dictionary of the English Language.*

23. Sharon Daloz Parks, *Big Questions, Worthy Dreams* (San Francisco: Jossey-Bass, 2000), 86–87.

24. Helgesen, *The Web of Inclusion,* 20.

25. Jean Lipman-Blumen, *The Connective Edge: Leading in an Interdependent World* (San Francisco: Jossey-Bass, 1990), 240.

26. Ibid., 230.
27. Ibid., 237.

Chapter 5: Bearing Religion

28. Miles Horton, with Judith Kohl and Herbert Kohl, *The Long Haul* (New York: Teachers College Press, 1998), x.
29. Ibid., 79–80.

Chapter 6: Finding the Words to Their Songs

30. Annie Dillard, "Write Till You Drop," *New York Times* book review section, May 28, 1989.
31. For full text and audio, see *www.americanrhetoric.com*.
32. Quoted in Sara Little, "'Experiments with Truth': Education for Leadership" in *Caring for the Commonweal: Education for Religious and Public Life*, ed. Parker J. Palmer, Barbara G. Wheeler, and James W. Fowler (Macon, GA: Mercer University Press, 1990), 178.
33. For more on the capacity to appreciate the truths of other faith traditions, see James W. Fowler, *Stages of Faith: The Psychology of Human Development and the Quest for Meaning* (San Francisco: Harper & Row, 1981).
34. Quoted in Helen Hunt, *Faith and Feminism* (New York: Atria Books, 2004), 103.

Chapter 7: Living a Seamless Life

35. Hunt, *Faith and Feminism*.

Chapter 8: A Palimpsest of Forces

36. Women in this study used double-negative phrases like this, as did those in a large study of people whose lives were devoted to the common good. See Laurent A. Parks Daloz et al., *Common Fire: Leading Lives of Commitment in a Complex World* (Boston: Beacon Press, 1996), chapter 7.
37. Samuel P. Oliner and Pearl M. Oliner, *The Altruistic Personality: Rescuers of Jews in Nazi Europe* (New York: Free Press, 1988).

38. Daloz et al., *Common Fire.*

39. Ibid., 255, note 14.

Chapter 9: Taking the Leap

40. Shibley Telhami, "Reflections of Hearts and Minds: Media, Opinion on Politics and Religion, and Identity in the Arab World," Jack and Lewis Rudin lecture at Auburn Theological Seminary, New York, May 10, 2005.

41. Paul Knitter, "The Eco-Human Crisis: Interfaith Dialogue and Global Responsibility," lecture given at the International Interfaith Centre, Oxford, England, November 1995.

42. Jonathan Sacks, *The Dignity of Difference: How to Avoid the Clash of Civilizations* (London: Continuum, 2002), 59–60.

43. Wilfred Cantwell Smith, *Towards a World Theology: Faith and the Comparative History of Religion* (Philadelphia: Westminster Press, 1981), 89.

44. Ibid., 44.

45. Sacks, *The Dignity of Difference,* 23.

46. *To the Contrary: A Discussion of Issues from a Variety of Women's Perspectives,* Public Broadcasting System. See "Women and Philanthropy: Sharing the Wealth" at *www.pbs.org/ttc/society/philanthropy.html.*

INDEX